BIBLE CHARACTERS AND DOCTRINES

Jairus to Blind Leaders

E. M. BLAIKLOCK, M.A., D.Litt.

Righteousness in Christ

WILLIAM L. LANE, Th.D.

William B. Eerdmans Publishing Company
Grand Rapids, Michigan

First Published 1973
First United States Edition January 1974

Printed in the United States of America

Library of Congress Cataloging in Publication Data
Main entry under title:

Bible characters and doctrines.

CONTENTS:
v. 3. Blaiklock, E. M. Nadab to Boaz. Wright, J. S.
The character of God.—v. 4. Blaiklock, E. M.
Elkanah to David. Grogan, G. The Holy Trinity.
v. 7. Blaiklock, E. M.
Uzziah to Daniel. Ellison, H. L. The life of Christ.
[etc.]
1. Bible—Study—Text-books. I. Blaiklock, E. M.
II. Wright, John Stafford. III. Grogan, Geoffrey.
BS605.2.B47 220'.07 72-189855

SCRIPTURE UNION IN NORTH AMERICA
U.S.A.: 1716 Spruce Street
Philadelphia, Pa. 19103
Canada: 5 Rowanwood Avenue, Toronto 5,
Ontario

INTRODUCTION

Each volume of Bible Characters and Doctrines is divided into the right number of sections to make daily use possible, though dates are not attached to the sections because of the books' continuing use as a complete set of character studies and doctrinal expositions. The study for each day is clearly numbered and the Bible passage to be read is placed alongside it.

Sections presenting the characters and doctrines alternate throughout each book, providing balance and variety in the selected subjects. At the end of each section there is a selection of questions and themes for further study related to the material covered in the preceding readings.

Each volume will provide material for one quarter's use, with between 91 and 96 sections. Where it is suggested that two sections should be read together in order to fit the three-month period, they are marked with an asterisk.

The scheme will be completed in four years. Professor E. M. Blaiklock, who writes all the character studies, will work progressively through the Old and New Testament records. Writers of the doctrinal sections contribute to a pattern of studies drawn up by the Rev. Geoffrey Grogan, Principal of the Bible Training Institute, Glasgow, in his capacity as Co-ordinating Editor. A chart overleaf indicates how the doctrinal sections are planned.

In this series biblical quotations are normally taken from the RSV unless otherwise identified. Occasionally Professor Blaiklock provides his own translation of the biblical text.

DOCTRINAL STUDY SCHEME

	Year 1	Year 2	Year 3	Year 4
First Quarter	The God who Speaks	Man and Sin	The Work of Christ	The Kingdom and the Church
Second Quarter	God in His World	Law and Grace	Righteousness in Christ	The Mission of the Church
Third Quarter	The Character of God	The Life of Christ	Life in Christ	The Church's Ministry and Ordinances
Fourth Quarter	The Holy Trinity	The Person of Christ	The Holy Spirit	The Last Things

DOCTRINAL STUDIES

RIGHTEOUSNESS IN CHRIST

Study		
The Broken Relationship		
1	Primal Sin	Genesis 3
2	The Power of a Lie	Psalm 53
3	The Mask of Religiosity	Isaiah 1
4	The Denial of God in Practice	Isaiah 59
5	Demonic Possession and Blasphemy	Matthew 12.22–37
6	The Peril of Materialism	Luke 12.13–21; 13.22–30
Justification in the Old Testament		
10	Faith and Justification	Genesis 15
11	Forgiveness and Justification	Psalm 32
12	Satisfaction and Justification	Isaiah 53.4–6, 10–12
13	Faithfulness and Justification	Habakkuk 1.12–2.5
Paul's Major Treatment of the Theme		
22	Righteousness Revealed	Romans 1.16–32
23	The Gentiles and the Just Judgement of God	Romans 2.1–16
24	The Jews and the Just Judgement of God	Romans 2.17–29
25	The Righteousness of God Challenged	Romans 3.1–20
26	The Righteousness of God Vindicated	Romans 3.21–31
27	Faith, Hope and the God who Raises the Dead	Romans 4
28	Righteousness Based on Faith	Romans 10.1–13
Justification Elsewhere in the New Testament		
36	Humility and Justification	Luke 18.9–17
37	The Quest for Eternal Life	Luke 18.18–30
38	Pardon or Peril	Acts 13.36–52
39	The Collapse of Self-confidence	Philippians 3.1–11
40	Faith Validated by Works	James 2.14–26

CHARACTER STUDIES

JAIRUS TO BLIND LEADERS

Study		
7	Jairus	Mark 5.21–43; Luke 8.41–56
8	The Woman in the Crowd	Luke 8.41–56; Romans 10.10–13
9	The Townsfolk	Mark 6.1–13; John 5.33–47
14	The Poor	Matthew 5.1–6; Isaiah 25
15	Those who Mourn	Matthew 5.4; Revelation 21.1–6; 22.1–7
16	The Meek	Matthew 5.5; 11.28–30; 26.47–54; Isaiah 42.1–4; 53.7
17	Those who Hunger and Thirst	Matthew 5.6; Psalm 119.105–120; Isaiah 55.1,2
18	The Merciful	Matthew 5.7; Proverbs 14.21, 22, 31; Colossians 3.12, 13
19	The Pure in Heart	Matthew 5.8; Psalm 51
20	The Peacemakers	Matthew 5.9; Isaiah 55; Ephesians 2.14–17
21	The Persecuted	Matthew 5.10–12; John 16.1–6; Revelation 7.9–17
29	The Salt of the Earth	Matthew 5.13–16; Genesis 18.16–33
30	Children of the Father	Matthew 5.17–48; John 10.1–13
31	The Hypocrite	Matthew 6.1–4; 23.13–36
32	The Man of Prayer	Matthew 6.5–7; 1 Kings 18.25–41
33	Child of the Father	Matthew 6.9–7.6; Acts 17.23–29; Luke 11.1–4
34	The Steadfast Petitioner	Matthew 7.7–23; Luke 11.5–13; Genesis 32.24–28
35	The Two Builders	Matthew 7.24–27; 1 Corinthians 3.9–28

Study		
41	Herod	Mark 6.14–29; John 3.19–36
42	Herodias	Matthew 14.1–14; Galatians 6.7, 8
43	Salome	Proverbs 28.1–18
44	Philip and Andrew	John 6.1–59
45	Child in the Crowd	Matthew 14.15–21; 26.26–30; Luke 9.10–17
46	The Crowd	Matthew 9.35–38; Mark 6.30–44
47	Greater than All	Matthew 10.32–42; 11.20–30; 12.1–8
48	The Way and the Truth	Matthew 12.38–42; John 12.44–50; 14.1–6
49	The Discoverers	Matthew 13.45, 46; John 6.60–69; Philippians 3.1–14
55	Characters of John's Gospel	John 1.1–18; 20.30, 31; 21.20–25
56	Wedding Guests	John 2.1–12; Exodus 20.1–12
57	Nicodemus	John 3.1–16; Ezekiel 36.25–27; 37.1–10
58	The Reborn	John 5.24; Romans 6.3–23
64	The Woman at the Well	John 4.1–30
65	The Samaritans	2 Kings 17.24–34; John 4.31–42; 8.48
66	Herod's Officer	John 4.43–54; Isaiah 55
67	The Man by the Pool	John 5.1–18
68	The Man in the Temple	John 5.19–29
76	The Crowd	John 7.17–44; 8.54–59; 11.54–57; 12.12–19
77	The Officers	John 7.45, 46; 18.1–8
78	Nicodemus	John 3.1–3; 7.50–53; 19.39–42
79	The Adulteress	John 3.17–21; 8.1–11
80	The Adulterer	John 8.12–44
81	The Man born Blind	John 9.1–12
82	The Man who Saw	John 9.13–41
83	Blind Leaders	Isaiah 42.6, 7, 18–20; 44.18–20; 53.1–3; John 9.39–41

RIGHTEOUSNESS IN CHRIST

The Broken Relationship

1 : Primal Sin

Genesis 3

We cannot adequately appreciate God's gracious provision of righteousness in Christ unless we first consider the extent of the rupture between God and man. Between Gen. **1**, **2** and Gen. **3** there exists the sharpest contrast. The man who was created in God's image as a creature-king and who was entrusted with the cultural mandate to exercise dominion over the earth and its creatures (Gen. **1**.26–28) is seen in Gen. **3**.8–10 cowering when he senses the presence of the Lord. Earlier he had been the delight of God and participated in the work of creation by naming the animals (Gen. **2**.18–20). Now he knows himself to be the object of God's displeasure, and he hides himself, experiencing the stark terror of the fugitive who has been hunted down. Disobedience to the mandate of the sovereign God induced guilt and anxiety, and reduced this formerly regal figure to the posture of a beaten slave. Adam and his wife were not content to be workers with God. They aspired to be 'like God' (5), to share equality of rank and dignity with Him. Self-deification is the heart of the primal sin, and lurks just beneath the surface of every sinful action. Only one who was 'like God' could choose to disregard His instruction. The free decision to listen to the voice of the Tempter and to trust him rather than the Creator accounts for the broken relationship between God and man.

The consequences of that rupture were immediate. In contrast to the state of being naked and unashamed (Gen. **2**.25), the man and the woman now experienced shame in the presence of their nakedness and hid themselves from each other (7). Having lost their joy in the presence of the Lord in the Garden, the man and his wife now hid themselves from Him, sensing that the coming of God no longer signified fellowship but judgement (8–10). The Bible knows nothing of the philosophers' concept of 'the hidden God', but only of the God who comes and of man who hides from His presence (cf. Rev. **6**.12–17). If God is hidden, it is sin that veils our egos. Adam hid himself from God, and from his wife who had been the gift of God. His experience of alienation from God inevitably affected his relationship to his wife; he blamed his fallen condition first on his wife and then on God ('the woman whom *thou* gavest to be with me . . .' 12). Pursuing the delusion that he could be like God, man exchanged the Garden for the uncultivated field choked by thistles and thorns, and the harmony of mutual delight for the bitterness of accusation and estrangement (16–19).

God's solemn judgement on man's bold act of self-affirmation shatters his fantasy. He is delivered over to the realm of death. He is dust, and unless the Spirit of God sustains him he will remain dust, and all he achieves will be blown away like a handful of dust (19). Prior to human disobedience the gift of God had been a person, the wife in whom the man delighted (Gen. **2**.21–23). Now God can give only things, garments to clothe his shame (21).

Adam is now a fugitive, and the presence of the guardian cherubim and the flaming sword blocking access to life (22–24) remain the tokens of the broken relationship. Yet even in their sorrow the man and his wife had the assurance that God would overcome the tragedy of their fall through 'the seed of the woman'. He will inflict a crushing wound on the serpent even though He must Himself be bruised (15). In this enigmatic promise, man was given the first clue that would lead him to God's costly provision of righteousness in Christ (cf. Rom. **16**.19 f. where the language of Gen. **3** recurs).

Question: *What are the signs of the fall which may appear even in the life of the Christian?*

2 : The Power of a Lie

Psalm 53

It is ironical that man disobeyed God in order to become wise (Gen. **3**.6)—only to experience utter foolishness (cf. Rom. **1**.21 f.). The serpent's promise that man would be 'like God' (Gen. **3**.5) was a lie, and believing a lie rather than the truth is the essence of foolishness. One lie spawns another, as the fool rids himself momentarily of God, his dangerous Adversary, by dismissing Him from all consideration. As an act of his will he affirms, 'There is no God' (1), in the delusion that wishing will make it so. His deeds stem from the conviction of his heart, and he abandons himself to corruption and depravity in the conviction that he must answer for his actions only to himself.

But God is not so easily dismissed. His reality is not dependent on our recognition and affirmation. He observes the entire human scene, prepared to recognize 'wisdom' as well as 'foolishness', where 'wisdom' is defined as seeking God (2) or calling upon Him (4). But the first man's disregard for God is repeated in the experience of every other man. The psalmist is emphatic that *all* men fall under the condemnation of the fool; no one does good or seeks God (3, cf. Rom. **3**.10–12). Foolishness and moral depravity are the bitter fruit of disobedience. The false promise of the Tempter was that man would know 'good and evil' (Gen. **3**.5), but in fact this psalm declares that he knows experientially only evil. The universality of human disobedience underscored by David indicates that men are unable to break their enslavement to the foolishness and corruption which resulted from their practical disregard for God and His mandates. Consequently, man preys on man (4)—as we can see all around us—and proves to be the manipulator and the manipulated, the victimizer and the victim. Yet for all his bold affirmation that there is no God, he experiences terror and shame, the evidence that God has rejected him (5). Deliverance can come only from God Himself if man is to be rescued from a living death.

David's deep disturbance over human depravity is clear, for Psa. **14** is virtually identical with Psa. **53**, with one important distinction. Psa. **14**.5 recognizes that 'God is with the generation of the righteous'. This fact sheds light on David's prayer for 'deliverance for Israel . . . from Zion' (Psa. **14**.7; **53**.6). God Himself must repair the broken relationship, restoring primal fellowship between Himself and men through an act of new creation. In this way He creates a generation of righteous men whose enjoyment of God will expose the utter folly of the fool's denial.

Thought: *Even as the actions of the fool display his*

commitment to a lie, the actions of the man of faith must demonstrate his commitment to the truth.

3 : The Mask of Religiosity

Isaiah 1

Isaiah has been called the evangelical prophet because he rarely pronounces a judgement or warns of punishment without presenting the offer of grace to those who will repent and trust the provision of God. This chapter exhibits the intimate connection between the sins and the suffering of the people, and summons them to judgement as the prelude to purification and deliverance.

Verses 2–9 expose the foolish rebellion of men, whose corruption stems from their broken relationship with God. The prophet caustically declares that even domestic animals, over which man was to rule, prove to be wiser than 'my own people' (3). His choice of nouns in v. 4 represents a careful progression (nation, people, offspring, sons) but each is qualified: 'a nation sinning, a people laden with iniquity, offspring of evil-doers, sons who act corruptly'. Filial ingratitude, inconsiderateness and habitual transgression express deep contempt for God. The cost of a spurned covenant relationship to God was acute suffering, personally and nationally, as Judah experienced invasion and ravaged cities (5–9).

Although Isaiah saw little distinction between Judah and the people of Sodom and Gomorrah (10), his contemporaries concealed their disregard for God behind a mask of religiosity. It is all too easy for us to follow their bad example. The second section of the prophecy (10–17) is a severe castigation of hypocrisy in religion. The sacrifices of the people were abundant, but unacceptable, their attendance at the Temple punctual, but insulting, because of iniquity (11–15). In a series of imperatives the prophet admonishes the nation to repent in intention and deed. God demands social justice and radical integrity (16 f.).

The heart of Isaiah's message details the gracious provision of God (18–23). With the same men who rebelled, and who disguised their rebellion beneath a religious mask, God enters into dialogue. He promises that even gross sin can be cleansed and forgiven, but demands the response of faith demonstrated through willing obedience. Continued rebellion invites only sustained judgement (20). The fall of the people from a state of righteousness to gross unrighteousness (21–23) prompts the promise of purification and deliverance for the remnant who will believe, but destruction for those who remain the enemies of God. Unrighteous counsellors will be replaced and the character of God's people as righteous and faithful will be vindicated through the provision of redemption by righteousness (25–27). Idolators who refuse to recognize His Lordship, however, will be consumed (28–31). God cannot disregard the rupture between Himself and men, and He will not tolerate the evasions of men satisfied with a false piety. He demands to be known as God and therefore summons men to receive righteousness as His free gift.

Thought: *God is uninterested in sacrifice or prayer which does not proceed from a cleansed heart.*

4 : The Denial of God in Practice

Isaiah 59

When a crisis occurs, we cry out to the Lord. When He fails to act and we are overwhelmed, inevitably we ask 'Why didn't God answer our prayers?' This anguished question is the occasion for Isaiah's sharp reprimand to his contemporaries. God is exonerated from all blame for the calamities that have overtaken Judah. The fault lies, not with the Lord, but with the people who have openly violated their covenant with God and now reap the harvest of their own sin. Sin always separates man from God and His protection (1 f.). The prophet accuses the people of rampant violence and injustice. He classified their acts as sins of the hands, mouth and feet (3–8), vividly suggesting that the whole body was engaged in reckless disregard for God and man. Murder, lying, judicial fraud and misrepresentation reflect the hardness of men conditioned to habitual evil. Their moral condition is one of darkness and hopeless degradation (9–15). In vs. 12 ff. the prophet confesses on behalf of the people that their actions constitute a blatant denial of God. We live in a different age and culture, but all these sins find expression in our own society.

This passage is the context to the important observation that persistence in sin actually restrains the breaking through of 'righteousness' (9, 14). In this instance 'righteousness' is equivalent to 'vindication', as the parallelism with 'salvation' in v. 11 indicates. There can be no redress of the evils that have overtaken the people until their own evil is rooted out and their relationship to God has been restored. God was horrified to see that there was no one who maintained His cause and who could intervene to halt the dissoluteness of the nation (15 b, 16). He therefore seized the initiative Himself, relying solely on His own 'righteousness' (where 'righteousness' in v. 16 is an attribute of God, in contrast to 'righteousness' as vindication in v. 11). As a warrior equipped for battle, God commits Himself to an adversary-relationship to His rebellious people and their oppressors (17–19). His intention, however, is redemptive. He will come to Zion as Redeemer, championing the cause of all those who will turn from transgressions in radical repentance (20; cf. Rom. **11**.26). The promise of salvation, in the high sense of release from sin and all its consequences, permits the summoning of the people to covenant renewal (21). By the sovereign action of God the broken relationship will be repaired and Israel will be restored to its privileged position as recipient and dispenser of the truth, sustained by the presence of the Holy Spirit.

5 : Demonic Possession and Blasphemy

Matthew 12.22–37

The healing of a blind and dumb demoniac exposes a darker consequence of the broken relationship between God and man, the enslavement of men to demonic powers. Jesus' engagement of the demonic, and His ability to release those who had been possessed, inevitably posed the question as to whether He was the agent of God's promised redemption (23). Yet certain Pharisees sought to discredit His activity as unlawful and dangerous. Their charge that Jesus cast out demons through collusion with the prince of the demonic kingdom (24) was utterly serious and bordered on blasphemy.

Jesus responded to their accusation through pithy proverbial sayings which exposed its fallacy: Satan is not able to cast out Satan (25 f.). By substituting 'Satan' for 'Beelzebul', Jesus brought the controversy explicitly within the perspective of His mission to engage the adversary of God in conflict. The expulsion of demons is nothing less than a forceful attack on Satan's dominion over men through possession, disease and death. Jesus' ability to cast out demons means that One stronger than Satan has come to restrain his activity and to release the enslaved. His mission is to confront Satan and to crush him on all fields, and in the fulfilment of His task He is conscious of being the agent of irresistible power. As the bearer of the Spirit, Jesus stands as the champion of God in the conflict with Satan (28 f.).

The expulsion of demons through the power of the Spirit signified the intrusion of God's sovereign redemptive activity. By ascribing the action of God to demonic origin, the Pharisees betrayed a perversion of spirit which, in defiance of the truth, chooses to call light darkness. This callousness of heart prompted Jesus' warning: blasphemy against the Holy Spirit denotes the conscious and deliberate rejection of the saving power and grace of God released through Jesus' liberating action. The considered judgement that Jesus' power was demonic betrayed a stubborn resistance to the Holy Spirit which exposes a man to grave peril. Jesus located the source of this resistance as an evil, unregenerate heart (33–35). The opposition of the Pharisees to Jesus and their eagerness to dissuade the people from following Him exhibited their perversion of spirit, for the spoken word accurately mirrors the condition of the heart. The sober warning that men will be judged by every careless word they have spoken (36 f.) heightens the demand that God Himself shall intervene to provide a righteousness in which a man may trust, for by his speech every man stands condemned.

Question: Are there aspects of your conversation that will change as you continue to reflect on the fact that every careless word will be recalled by God on the day of judgement?

6 : The Peril of Materialism

Luke 12.13–21; 13.22–30

A major effect of the broken relationship is an inversion of priorities. Unable to delight himself in God man finds himself incapable of delight in himself or another as a person. His delight is only in the accumulation of objects which become for him the measure of his security and success. Rejecting the possession of God, he becomes a materialist, with an obsession to possess things. Even the people who enter his life are treated as objects to be used instead of persons to be enjoyed. Surrounded by objects over which he exercises mastery, he can maintain the delusion that he is the sovereign of his life. He can play at being 'like God' (Gen. **3**.5). Selfishness, greed, and material idolatry follow as a natural consequence.

Jesus warned that a man's life cannot be evaluated by the abundance of his material possessions (15). The parable of a wealthy land-owner who enjoyed more prosperity than he anticipated (16–20), illustrates His point. This man's commitment to materialism led him to make three tragic mistakes. 1. He mistook his body for his soul (19). He measured the needs of his life only in terms of food and drink and so was convinced he possessed everything necessary to enjoy life. 2. He mistook man for God. Believing he was the master of his own life, he did not hesitate to relax in his comfortable circumstances (19). Accustomed to making decisions, he knew immediately what he would do with his bumper crop (18). But there is sobering irony in the contrast between vs. 18 and 20: 'He said . . . but God said . . .'. 3. He mistook time for eternity. He believed he had ample provision 'for many years' (19), but God appointed 'this night' (20) as the time of his death. Concerned only with material wealth, he neglected and forfeited his life. He allowed himself to be lulled into a sense of false security by his abundant possessions and so played the fool. The price of the neglect of God is always the death of the human spirit.

Jesus taught that the possession of God now is the condition of enjoying Him for ever. A man can be 'rich toward God' (21) only if he reorders his priorities so that the knowledge of God as Lord becomes pre-eminently important to him. That is the significance of Jesus' counsel to 'strive to enter' life 'by the narrow door' (Luke **13**.24). There will be a terrible separation of those who have presumed that they knew God (26) from those who have acknowledged His lordship over their lives in an absolute sense, who will share banquet-fellowship with Him (28 f.). The refusal to submit to God as sovereign Lord now inexorably brings a man to the moment when God will not acknowledge him (25–27). This is the great reversal to which the broken relationship consigns many who now enjoy congratulation for their position and prestige. It makes imperative an understanding of God's provision of righteousness in Christ.

Thought: Those who will not pray, 'Thy will be done', will one day hear God say to them, 'Your will be done'!

Questions and themes for study and discussion on Studies 1–6

1. Read your daily newspaper for a week, collecting evidence of the broken relationship. Attempt to discern the theological significance of current events.
2. What evidence of estrangement and broken relationships can you find in your own home? Does Gen. **3** shed any light on the resolution of conflicts?
3. When the 'God is Dead' theologians broke into print a few years ago they attracted considerable attention. Does anything positive result from such 'disturbances' to the Church?
4. A popular statement runs, 'What you do speaks so loud that I cannot hear what you say'. Is it possible for the people of God to obscure the reality of the Lord by their behaviour at the same time as they are devoting themselves to evangelism and mission?
5. Intellectual debate rarely convinces an unbeliever of God's reality or of his own need for God's gracious provision of righteousness in Christ. How may these truths be effectively communicated?
6. To what can the vigorous interest in Satan and the occult in contemporary culture be attributed? Is it wise for a Christian to concern himself with this renewed interest in the demonic?
7. What is the evidence that a materialistic concern always imperils a sensitive pursuit of matters of the Spirit?

CHARACTER STUDIES

7 : Jairus

Mark 5.21–43; Luke 8.41–56

Jairus' story is told more fully in Mark than in either Matthew or Luke. Mark had the facts from Peter, and Peter had seen Jairus' agony at first hand, being one of those taken into the dead child's room. Follow the ordeal of the good Jairus. Jesus had arrived unexpectedly, at what time we do not know. The party had possibly drifted across the lake in the night, and had appeared on the western shore early on the following morning.

News soon spread. The whole lake, on its Jewish west and its Greek east, was thickly populated. Jairus must have thought it an amazing answer to prayer. He came urgently to Christ and fell at His feet. His plea was heard, and the Lord accompanied him up the narrow, crowded street. The unfeeling crowd, greedy for wonder, gathered round and blocked the way. Progress was agonizingly slow. He must have seemed to the distraught and tormented Jairus not to care. And he had said that his little one lay 'at the point of death'. So often when He really plans to give more than we have asked, does God seem to wait and not to hear.

Then the worst happened. Progress had been slow enough as the little group thrust through the impeding multitude, but now it stopped altogether. And for whom? Not for a dying child, but for a woman, a woman, Jairus would think, selfishly preoccupied with her inconsiderable ill while his 'little daughter lay at the point of death'—the point of death! The words hammered his mind. And he had told Jesus as much.

And now the dreaded messenger—too late, the end had come, and all perhaps, because of that shuffling progress, that selfish crowd, that woman . . . Jairus was crushed, but the Lord turned to him and quenched his fear. 'Only believe'. How impossible a word it seemed! But the scene in the room of death revealed the full significance. It was one of those moments which burn a picture and a memory into the brain. Peter remembered the very words: 'Talitha kumi'.

Jairus received 'far more abundantly' than all he asked or thought. Jairus had known crushing agony. He now knew why God had permitted him so desperately to suffer. Thus, sometimes, with life.

As when Lazarus died, the Lord was well aware of the deep distress of those He loved, but He had more to give them than the boon for which they prayed. 'Did I not tell you that if you would believe you would see the glory of God?' Jairus was to see the glory of God and to praise the Lord for His delay all the rest of his life. Men are sometimes called to endure that which appears to surpass all limits. Let it fortify the soul to know that He sees, and knows, and has not lost control. Beyond what men count catastrophe lies 'the glory of God'.

8 : The Woman in the Crowd

Luke 8.41–56; Romans 10.10–13

Look now at Luke's account. The physician leaves out the pungent phrase at the end of Mark **5**.26, in which we almost hear the downright Peter's very voice as he told Mark the story. Moved by a deep and urgent hope, which proved the father of faith, she thrust through the crowd until she was near enough to insinuate a hand and touch the hem of His robe. A surge of health told her she was healed.

But with that sensitivity which was part of His uncorrupted body Jesus knew that He had given something of Himself, some of the boundless life that was His to give. Hence the question which was so baffling to the disciples, who, at that tense moment, were perhaps sharing the pain and haste of poor Jairus.

She 'fell down before him, and told him the whole truth' (Mark **5**.33). It is pointless in all our relations with Christ to do anything less—or to imagine that a healing contact with Him can leave us lost and faceless in the crowd. Inevitably she was drawn out of the multitude and compelled to identify herself in public with the One who had conferred His blessing upon her.

The woman in the crowd becomes therefore an example. There are those who in diffidence, in shyness or in hesitation seek to limit contact. They desire the touch of His healing, but they are reluctant to stand out and be numbered with Him. Fear and trembling (Mark 5.33) are maladies of the mind to which many sensitive souls are subject, but they are ills which, like the damage to our soul which His touch can heal and forgive, must be brought into reach of His blessed hands.

It is *with* Christ that a man finds his peace, his standing and his usefulness. The preposition matters. To be sure other prepositions are valid and contain their truths. Blessing comes *in* Christ, *through* Christ, *by* Christ . . . but it is *with* Christ, identified, conspicuous, strong, like the house on the rock, that the committed Christian must stand. We are safe nowhere else. It is thus that we 'go in peace' and know our malady no more.

I am trusting Thee for pardon!
At Thy feet I bow,
For Thy grace and tender mercy
Trusting now.

I am trusting Thee, Lord Jesus;
Never let me fall;
I am trusting Thee for ever,
And for all.

—(Frances Ridley Havergal)

9 : The Townsfolk

Mark 6.1–13; John 5.33–47

We have been following Mark over some of these events, and now we meet the people of Nazareth again, among whom Christ could do no significant work of good. It is interesting to look at the Lord's townsfolk and see why this terrible impotence was manifest. God's grace is touched to effectiveness by faith. It is thrust upon none in despite of the will.

In a letter written from Pavia during his mission there, the Florentine reformer Savanarola explained to his mother why he was working in distant Lombardy: 'Seeing that He has chosen me for this sacred task, be content that I fulfil it far from my native place, for I bear better fruit than I could have borne at home. There it would be with me as it was with Christ, when His countrymen said: Is not this the son of Joseph the carpenter? But out of my own place this has never been said to me; rather, when I have to depart, men and women shed tears, and hold my words in much esteem'. It was a common bush which flamed with glory for Moses. One who sought less urgently for God's will might have seen nothing strange. This was Mrs Browning's point:

Earth's crammed with heaven
And every common bush afire with God;
But only he who sees takes off his shoes,
The rest sit round it and pluck blackberries,
And daub their natural faces unaware
More and more from the first similitude.

God is revealed to those who seek Him. Those whose heart and mind are set on self, who deliberately confine ambition and desire to the world and the flesh, can persuade themselves that the very words of Christ contain no wonder, that Creation can be dismissed as chance, that conscience itself is the product of chemical changes in the body. In other words, it is those who seek who find. Let but the soul cry out for relief and light, and the glory of God begins to glimmer in Nature, in the Scriptures, in Christ.

In a sense it is Gadara again, perhaps with less excuse. In the Decapolis town they were preoccupied with their pig-farming. In Nazareth, Jews not Greeks, the dull townsmen of the Lord were preoccupied each with himself, unable in sheer dullness of heart and mind to see any beauty or appeal in One whom they had seen with plane and chisel in hand at work before a local bench. And so they missed, like the Gadarenes, the glory of the Christ.

Questions and themes for study and discussion on Studies 7–9

1. The meaning of pain and God's delays in the story of Jairus.
2. What of secret discipleship in the light of Mark 5.30?
3. The people of Nazareth and Gadara and their counterparts today.

RIGHTEOUSNESS IN CHRIST

Justification in the Old Testament

10 : Faith and Justification

Genesis 15

Although Abraham was severely tested, God gave to him the priceless gift of a strong and vigorous faith. When calling him from Haran, God promised that he would possess the land, that he would have descendants, and that he would be a blessing to the nations (Gen. **12**.1–3). Yet no part of the promise had as yet been fulfilled. God's appearance to Abram in a vision was to reassure him that he enjoyed divine protection and that his reward would be great (1). His trust was to be in the person of God, his hope in the promise of God. Abram's spirited response indicates that his thoughts were narrowly focused on God's original promise of an heir. Among the Hurrians a childless man might adopt an heir to ensure his proper burial, but Abram found no comfort in the thought that his steward, a household slave, would become his heir (2 f.). His reply was an expression of faith, not unbelief, and was honoured by the explicit pledge of vs. 4 f. The starry sky provided a visible word or sign that brought the promise of a son into sharp focus, and Abram 'believed God' (6). He placed his confidence solely on God's achievement. As an expression of sovereign grace, God received this informal faith as righteousness and justified Abram, i.e. He treated him as righteous.

Verse 6 is twice cited by Paul (Rom. **4**.3; Gal. **3**.6) and once by James (**2**.23) to confirm that justification has always been by faith. Faith in this context is the readiness to accept what God promises. It is not presented as a crowning merit, as if Abram's ability to believe God was due to inherent character. His faith was summoned by the grace of God. Abram trusted, not in himself, but in the goodness and faithfulness of God to do what He had promised.

That the ground of Abram's justification was not his believing, but God's free and gracious decision, is confirmed in vs. 7–21. There the promise concerning the land is clarified and strengthened by the inauguration of a formal covenant. The covenantal ritual (9 f.) calls to mind Jer. **34**.18: ordinarily both parties to a covenant between men would pass through the dismembered animals to invoke dismemberment for themselves should they break their covenant pledge. Here Abram's part is only to prepare the sacrifice and to guard it from violation (11). Dread and great darkness (12) signalled the presence of the Lord, and convey the impact of holiness upon sin. The smoke and the fire (17) appear to have been a theophany, a visible manifestation of God. He alone ratified the covenant (17 f.), so that it will be understood that the ordering of covenant fellowship between a righteous God and justified man belongs solely with Him. The accent falls on two integral components of justification in the Old Testament, God's initiative and His free act of giving.

Thought: Like the covenant with Abraham, the New Covenant was inaugurated in darkness (*Matt.* **27**.45).

11 : Forgiveness and Justification

Psalm 32

Supreme joy is appropriate to one who has felt the full weight of his sins and who, through repentance and confession, has received divine forgiveness and reconciliation. This psalm is attributed to David and is intelligible in the light of his experience with gross sin (2 Sam. **11**). Although his conscience would allow him no peace, he refused to acknowledge his sins. Only the accusation of Nathan (2 Sam. **12**.1 ff.) reduced him to the repentance and confession expressed in Psa. **51.** Psa. **32** is a shout of praise from a man who has been forgiven and restored to fellowship with God. The experience described is common to all those who have known the painfulness of guilt and anxiety, and the joy of forgiveness and restoration.

David labels his actions as transgression, sin, and iniquity (1 f.). Transgression is a deliberate violation of God's commandment as an act of wilful self-assertion; sin implies a wandering from the way; iniquity signifies a perverse turning aside from the proper course of action. In the experience of forgiveness God lifted the heavy load of his transgression and completely removed it; He covered the foulness of his sin, so that it no longer cried out for divine judgement; and He kept no judicial record of his past iniquity. By His gracious action God deals with the offender as if he had been without offence. This is the startling character of justification. Yet divine forgiveness is extended only to one in whom there is no deceitfulness. Unless the attempt to deceive self or God is abandoned in a resolute refusal to deny or conceal, extenuate or excuse sinfulness, there can be no justification or restoration of the sinner.

This realization was slow in coming. David refused to acknowledge his sin to himself or to God, and experienced the wretchedness of a joyless and broken life (3 f.). His body ached in sympathy with the distress of his soul until he realized that his acute suffering was the result of unconfessed and unforgiven sin. Sin is destructive to the body and mind of a man as well as to his spirit, as our newspapers show us every day. Conversely, the removal of sin and guilt through repentance and confession is a healing experience, releasing a man to life. David finally recognized the futility of maintaining his silence, and uncovered his sinful life before God in an act of complete confession. Then he received the assurance that God had removed his guilt and had forgiven him (5). This is the blessedness of which he speaks in vs. 1 f., and furnishes the ground of the exhortation to prayer in a time of distress in vs. 6 f. The man who has been justified by God will find his security in the Lord, even when his life has been deeply involved in sin. In the prayer of penitence and supplication he will experience the forgiveness of God and will be guarded from the distress of sin which is common to those who do not know the Lord (6 f.). He may count on the instruction of the Lord who will teach him that submission which preserves a man from repeated sin (8 f.). Out of his own past experience David is able to bear witness to the anguish of the wicked who resist the promptings of God and the gladness of those who trust in the covenant faithfulness of the Lord (10 f.).

Thought: *Sin must be 'uncovered' by me before it can be 'covered' by God.*

12 : Satisfaction and Justification

Isaiah 53.4–6, 10–12

Through the provision of righteousness God rescues men from the eternal death merited by their sin. The costliness of that provision is the theme of Isa. **53** with its presentation of the Servant of the Lord whose suffering and death satisfied divine justice and made possible the justification of the many. The passage develops the contrast between the One who is righteous and who becomes the source of righteousness to others, and the many who possess no righteousness apart from Him. Ironically, men regarded the Servant as One punished by God on His own account, so loathsome were the griefs and sorrows He bore (4). In an act of vicarious suffering He took upon Himself, as though they were His own, sicknesses which properly belonged to us and which we deserved to bear, in order that we might be delivered from them. Yet when we saw Him laden with affliction we failed to understand, but persisted in the mistaken notion that He was the just object of God's wrath.

The depth of error in this judgement is exposed in the contrast between the 'we' of v. 4 and the 'He' of v. 5, and by the clear statement of substitutionary atonement in the satisfaction of divine justice in vs. 5 f. The two verbs used in v. 5, 'pierced through' (translated 'wounded') and 'crushed' (translated 'bruised'), are among the strongest expressions in the Hebrew language to denote a violent and painful death. The blow merited by our transgressions has fallen not on us but on the Servant, freeing us from the consequences of our sin. When He assumed the chastisement due to us He rendered satisfaction and secured for us peace with God. The barriers which had kept God from being at peace with us were removed, so that we might enjoy a right relationship with Him (cf. Isa. **57**.19; Eph. **2**.13–18). The healing of our brokenness, however, was costly, for men do not themselves possess the ability to atone for their sins. What men could not do, God has done through the vicarious suffering and death of His Servant who died in their place. Substitutionary suffering lies at the heart of God's provision of justification, even as self-centredness and lostness lie at the heart of man's need. This is evident in the structure of v. 6 which begins and ends in the Hebrew with the words 'all of us'. 'All of us' had sinned, but the Lord intervened and laid upon the Servant the burden of the iniquity of 'all of us'.

The ultimate cause of the Servant's sufferings was God Himself. It was His will to bruise His Servant, because His death was designed to expiate sin. When the Servant makes His life a trespass offering, satisfaction for sin is achieved (10). The primary idea of the guilt or trespass offering was the satisfaction of indebtedness which released the sinner from his guilt (cf. Lev. **5**). As a righteous Priest the Servant freely offers His life as a righteous sacrifice for sins (cf. Heb. **9**.26). Because He did so voluntarily, He is promised abundant satisfaction (11). Death is unable to hold Him; He will live again and His life becomes the Source of life for those whose guilt He has removed in His death. By knowing Him, many shall be justified since He took away their iniquity. Because He suffered for others in this unique sense, He is appointed to a place of unparalleled honour. The prophecy closes with God's declaration of the extent of the Servant's victory and a review of His sufferings (12). He stands as the Victor among those who have been justified by His submission, who remain the objects of His ministry of intercession (cf. Heb. **7**.23–25).

Thought: *Those who know that the terrible burden of sin has been removed, look with gratitude and devotion to the cross where the guilt of sin was once borne by Jesus, the suffering Servant of the Lord.*

13 : Faithfulness and Justification

Habakkuk 1.12–2.5

In the alternating structure of prophetic complaint and divine response, the prophecy of Habakkuk focuses on two types of men, the presumptuous ('not upright') man and the man of faith (**2**.4). The presumptuous man is probably Nebuchadnezzar, while the faithful man is the prophet himself. A man of deep feeling, he is learning to trust God, although he clearly had problems in understanding why evil was allowed to go unchecked and unpunished. He observed an absence of justice, the people were full of violence and discord, the land was in a shambles, and he complained that God appeared to be indifferent (**1**.1–4). When God replied that He was neither indifferent nor inactive, for He was bringing the Babylonians to invade Judah as the instrument of His judgement (**1**.5–11), the prophet's sense of justice was outraged. How can God use a wicked nation to punish His people (**1**.12–**2**.1)? Is not God's own justice violated by this course of events when men more righteous than the Babylonians will be sacrificed to their cruel lust for conquest (**1**.13) while the presumptuous man is confirmed in his arrogance (**1**.14–17)? The prophet's retirement in quietness of spirit is the proper preparation for hearing the word of the Lord.

God's reply, that the purging of His people is necessary, must be viewed in the perspective of His sovereignty (**2**.1–20). That God's ordained acts are sometimes *against* His people, but *for* their higher good, is a hard truth that can be grasped only if you possess the vision of God's majesty which informs Habakkuk's song in praise of the Lord in ch. **3**. The promise that the earth will be filled with the knowledge of the glory of the Lord (**2**.14) prompts the prophet's prayer that God will revive His work *in history*, so that His glory may be perceived in the earth (**3**.2). The heart of the reply is the recognition of the presumption of the ungodly man and the fidelity of the upright man (**2**.4). This distinction assumes the intervention of God in the historical process for the redemption of His people (**2**.2 f.). Opposed to the presumptuous self-sufficiency of men who recklessly impose their will on the nations is radical faith in the God who proves Himself. The righteous man must learn to live by his faithfulness and steadfast endurance (cf. Heb. **10**.38). God is absolutely trustworthy, and His faithfulness is reproduced in those who place their confidence in Him. Such faithfulness distinguishes the company of the justified from those who rely only on their own strength (cf. Rom. **1**.17; Gal. **3**.11). Habakkuk's own faith in God's gracious and sovereign provision is beautifully expressed in the confession of **3**.17–19. Justification is appropriated through faith and issues in faithfulness.

Thought: *Is it possible to see God at work in the activities of the great powers in today's world?*

Questions and themes for study and discussion on Studies 10–13

1. Is Abraham's boldness with God to be reflected in our own relationship with Him? What is required of the man who is bold toward God?
2. Make a list of those promises of God that you are eager for Him to fulfil. Consider any conditions associated with them and then see if you can claim those promises through prayer.
3. What evidence is there in your own experience that guilt erodes human relationships as well as one's relationship with God? Is it the Christian's responsibility to forgive unacknowledged sin?
4. Using the New Testament as your guide, reflect on the extent to which Jesus fulfilled the prophecy of Isa. **53.** Be specific. How would you explain Isa. **53** to a Jewish friend?
5. Does it seem to you that God has relaxed His hold on the course of national and international events? Can you discern any evidence that God continues to manifest His lordship in modern history?

CHARACTER STUDIES

14 : The Poor

Matthew 5.1–6; Isaiah 25

We do not know just when, in the early ministry of the Lord, the words of the Sermon on the Mount were uttered. Perhaps, like most good sermons, this famous discourse was given more than once. Luke says that the same words were heard on level ground (**6**.17), perhaps to those unable to climb, or out of hearing. Some say that the sermon was given to the Twelve only. If so, the Sermon on the Plain, to which Luke makes reference, certainly had a larger audience. Nor does it look as if the occasion described by Matthew (**5**.1) was a scene of retreat.

At any rate, the Lord began with the preoccupation of Psa. **1**—'Who is the happy man?' He began with the poor, and ended, as paradoxically, with the persecuted. Matthew, to be sure, renders the Lord's Aramaic by 'the poor in spirit', Luke says simply 'the poor', but it is all one. The poor were poor in spirit.

Sir George Adam Smith, in his great study of Isa. **25**, writes movingly on the theme. He points out that in the East poverty meant more than mere physical disadvantage. The poor man was too often, in popular religion, considered the God-forsaken man. The poor man lay under Heaven's frown, deprived because he merited deprivation. And commonly this is what he himself believed. It thus came about that the poor man was deprived of justice, respect, acceptance. He was lonely, burdened in heart, in a word 'poor in spirit'.

He hungered, therefore, for God, for justice, for love, as well as for food. And, says the commentator, 'it was by developing, with the aid of God's Spirit, this quick conscience and this deep desire for God, which in the East are the very soul of physical poverty, that the Jews advanced to the sense of evangelical poverty of heart, blessed by Jesus in the first of His Beatitudes, as the possession of the Kingdom of Heaven.'

Hence, for the Remnant—the choice among them—the worth and the lessons of the Exile when the whole nation, the noble, the saintly, the gentle, the cultured, priest, soldier, citizen, woman, youth and child, were torn from home and estate, deprived of standing, liberty and all that which had seemed the mark of God's favour, and were led to the discovery that in such degradation and bereavement God cared. So 'the poor in spirit', no longer arrogant, purged of materialism, became the meek, and the humble, asking of God nothing more than His righteousness. And so Christ gives dignity, worth, meaning to suffering, and causes the poor in spirit to see that in His sight they stand higher than the proud, the self-sufficient and the rich of this ephemeral world.

15 : Those who Mourn

Matthew 5.4; Revelation 21.1–6; 22.1–7

The Exile taught the faithful of Israel the true meaning of pain. We saw Job wrestle with that theme, and Habakkuk, too. And now the Lord numbers among the happy breed 'those that mourn'. The significance of sorrow is the most difficult of all life's lessons to learn. Sorrow can paralyse and embitter. It can also sanctify, and the Lord meant that they are blessed who face the opportunity to draw closer to Him in the school of stress and grief.

These are words which it requires courage to write. The Lord Himself permits us to pray that we be not led into testing, for that is one meaning of 'temptation'. On the other hand, life being as it is, somewhere, at some time, we must face the tutelage of sorrow. Perhaps we should ask ourselves whether we can grow to full stature without it. 'As long as man remains as he is,' writes Hugh Silvester, 'a world without pain, disappointments, obstructions and frustrations might well lead to such an increase of arrogance and hardness of heart that life would become insupportable. The world as it is appears to be the only suitable home for man as he will be.'

It is a lesson which has broken through to many. Oscar Wilde in his moving book *De Profundis*, wrote over seventy years ago from his prison cell at Reading: 'I used to live entirely for pleasure. I shunned suffering and sorrow of every kind. I hated both. I resolved to ignore them as far as possible; to treat them; that is to say, as modes of imperfection. They were not part of my scheme of life. But my mother, who knew life as a whole, used to quote to me Goethe's lines . . .,

Who never ate his bread in sorrow,
Who never spent his midnight hours
Weeping and waiting for the morrow—
He knows you not, ye heavenly powers.

Oscar Wilde read his Greek Testament in Reading Jail, but Matthew's verse never got to the centre of his being and his sorrow. But there it stands, for our challenge, and for our faith: 'Happy are those who mourn—for they shall be comforted.' And the comfort of God is comfort indeed.

16 : The Meek

Matthew 5.5; 11.28–30; 26.47–54; Isaiah 42.1–4; 53.7

It is difficult not to linger with the characters of the Sermon on the Mount. It is good to do so, and to grow to understand them, for they never walked the earth—save one. When Plato, over five centuries before Christ spoke, wrote his *Republic*, that ten-volume work on the ideal state, he ended with words tinged with sadness. It is a state, he said, 'planted in imagination, for I conceive it nowhere on earth . . . in heaven there is perhaps a pattern of it, stored up for any man who wishes to see it . . .'

So it is with the happy men and women of the Beatitudes. Only Christ fulfilled the pattern perfectly, but it is a pattern 'stored up in heaven for any man who wishes to see it . . .' That is why we must look at these 'characters of Scripture', and know them.

What is meekness? It is suffering wrong without bitterness. It is not insensitivity, unmanliness, servility. It neither cringes nor whines. It lies in the patience of Christ, in forbearance. It feels pain but not malice. It is the quality of love, which 'bears all things'. It is both active and passive, in that it not only endures, but does good. It rests on self-control, abjures self-pity, turns from petty revenge, maintains righteousness, and never harms another. It is a fountain of true life, 'for the wound which is borne in God's way brings a change of heart too salutary to regret; but the hurt that is borne in the world's way brings death' (2 Cor. 7.10, NEB).

Moses, we read, was 'a meek man', and among the characters of the Old Testament there was no man more strong, brave, and effective in his leadership. The secret lies in Psa. **37**, the eleventh verse of which the Lord quoted in this saying. And that psalm was a psalm of patience and blessed quietness, of the still mind which refuses to fret and fume at the transient triumphs of the evildoers, that rests in the Lord, and meanwhile works at the ever-ready tasks of goodness, righteousness and love.

Put these qualities together into a human personality, and you have the meek man—or Jesus Christ our Lord.

17 : Those who Hunger and Thirst

Matthew 5.6; Psalm 119.105–120; Isaiah 55.1, 2

It is obvious through all the Bible that no benediction rests upon half-heartedness. Lot's wife looked back and died. The prophets burned with desire to do God's will. A single-hearted devotion breaks through the whole anthology of Psa. **119**. The Lord turned away the disciples who came with reservations. No blessing awaits the uncommitted. That is what the fourth Beatitude means.

Its metaphor must be seen in its context of time and place. Few of those who read these pages really know what hunger is. The land in which Christ lived was a poverty-stricken land. The great sheet of the Galilee lake lay before Him as He spoke, with Tiberias straight ahead down its eastern shore. The fishermen of the lakeside towns enjoyed a measure of prosperity but in the little towns and villages of Galilee and Judea and in the back-streets of Tiberias itself, was destitution not to be found in Western lands today. Calcutta may show such pockets of misery. So may other towns in ill-favoured lands where multitudes lack work and bread.

There were those who heard Christ who knew what hunger was, hunger that made men desperate, obsessed with one desire. Such is the desire for good, for God, for righteousness which finds fulfilment and satisfaction. Set it beside our tepid devotion and half-hearted goodness.

And thirst . . . To know consuming thirst is perhaps a more common experience. Thirst that makes clean, cool water look the most beautiful sight on earth, thirst that is an importunate desire. This is the desire which wins its satisfaction—

The thirst that from the soul doth rise
Doth ask a drink divine . . .

Ben Jonson's lyric was correct in a wider sense than he intended . . . 'My soul thirsts for thee,' wrote David (Psa. 63.1), 'my flesh faints for thee, as in a dry and weary land where no water is.' Those words sprang from one who, a hunted refugee in the wadis and canyons of Judea's wilderness, knew the pain of the body's deprivation, and saw in his distress the very image of the passion with which he longed for the will of God, manifest in his life and his salvation. The world needs such men and women, needs them desperately, for we live in the age which Yeats described in his grim poem—

The best lack all conviction,
While the worst are full of passionate intensity.

Question: Was Yeats right in his description?

18 : The Merciful

Matthew 5.7; Proverbs 14.21, 22, 31; Colossians 3.12, 13

Few words of Shakespeare are better known than Portia's speech in *The Merchant of Venice*. The great dramatist was never closer to the New Testament than when he wrote those lines . . .

The quality of mercy is not strain'd,
It droppeth as the gentle rain from heaven
Upon the place beneath: it is twice blest;
It blesseth him that gives and him that takes:
'Tis mightiest in the mightiest: it becomes
The throned monarch better than his crown;
His sceptre shows the force of temporal power,
The attribute to awe and majesty,
Wherein doth sit the dread and fear of kings;
But mercy is above this sceptred sway;
It is enthroned in the hearts of kings,
It is an attribute to God himself;

Perhaps mercy is more easy to demonstrate than meekness, though the two are allied, for mercy, though it is equally an attitude and a quality, shows itself more sharply in specific acts of generous forgiveness.

Mercy is God's grace reflected in human conduct, just as it is God's grace in action towards man. In showing mercy, as Shakespeare said, we most closely imitate the Living God;

in denying it, we most surely betray Him, for as Blake put it. 'Mercy has a human heart, Pity a human face'. He surely meant that men see both qualities and comprehend them both in merciful and pitiful actions by men and women of Christ's mould. To grant mercy or to withhold, is surely in man's power. Dryden was right:

Reason to rule, but mercy to forgive:
The first is law, the last, prerogative.

The thought is awesome. At the point of time when a call to show the divine quality of mercy comes, perhaps at that point a man demonstrates whether or not he knows the grace of God. Is the unmerciful man a Christian at all? Is the merciful man 'blessed', because in showing mercy, he proves his Christian standing? Does the latter half of the verse support this thought? It is not in this world that the merciful receive always in return the mercy they have shown. The merciful have died for mercy's sake. Consider Calvary . . .

We have quoted three poets. Let us quote a fourth as a final prayer. It is Alexander Pope:

Teach me to feel another's woe,
To hide the fault I see;
That mercy I to others show,
That mercy show to me.

19 : The Pure in Heart

Matthew 5.8; Psalm 51

The sixth Beatitude is a challenging word, if ever there was one. The word translated 'pure' means 'unadulterated', 'unmixed', 'uncomplicated' by admixture of alien elements. It is, as Augustine put it, a heart which is *simplex*. We have the word 'simple' from that Latin word, but the Latin word is a much wider word than its derivative. It means, according to the daunting list in the Latin dictionary, 'without dissimulation, open, frank, straightforward, direct, guileless, honest, sincere . . .'

Simplex is the opposite to *duplex* from which we derive no corresponding adjective, but a very unsavoury noun—duplicity. *Simplex* means 'having only one fold', whereas *duplex* means basically 'folded twice' as though to conceal the contents. Virtue, it implies, can be calculating, with hidden motives which, in God's eyes, destroy its worth. It can be contaminated with pride, ambition, deceit. True goodness has no other desire than to do the will of God.

Hence the qualifying phrase. It is the 'pure in heart' who meet God face to face, and know Him as a man knows his friend. 'Heart' is a common metaphor in both Testaments. It means the core of the personality, that inner man, that depth within us where the real person is, where conscience dwells, where God's Spirit finds entry or exclusion. The 'desires of our heart' (Psa. **37**.4) are what the true Christian, in his moments of deepest sincerity, wants from God. The 'inward being' of David's agonized prayer (Psa. **51**.6) found definition in the same context (**51**.10). He knew where the vast tragedy began. He had allowed the citadel of his being to be penetrated long before he looked down from his roof and saw Bathsheba.

What lies at the core seeps outward into the whole. The 'inward being' contains that which finds ultimate expression in word and thought. The whole becomes ultimately what that inward part determines. The 'pure in heart' are the blessed ones who have set utter holiness in the centre of the person, and who else can take it to that all-important sanctuary save Christ? The pure in conduct will find ultimate defeat if in some decaying room lurks the impurity which cannot be contained but, like some feebly concealed and poisoned waste, escapes and corrupts the whole.

List references to 'the heart' from both Testaments.

20 : The Peacemakers

Matthew 5.9; Isaiah 55; Ephesians 2.14–17

Raymond Gram Swing, whose name was known in the middle decades of the century for his broadcast comments on international affairs, remarked of the times we live in: 'The peace we enjoy is the absence of war, rather than the presence of confidence, understanding and generous conduct'.

The peace of God is not this pale and negative state. It begins in the heart when Christ is enthroned there, and then, like the 'well of water springing up to everlasting life', it flows into the environment. The peacemakers are those whose presence and whose fellowship draw men into right relationships. There are those who, by their very nature, are promoters of strife. And they are promoters of strife because they are creatures of strife. The personality of man is no sealed container. That which lies at the heart's core seeps out and permeates the environment, be it good or evil. And that is why they only can make peace in whose heart peace reigns.

To make peace is not to impose peace, much less to destroy all opposition. 'They make a desert and they call it peace', Tacitus, the great Roman historian, makes a British chieftain say. This is not God's peace. Nor is God's peace bought at any price, for it is not acquiescence in wrong which demands resistance, it is not disregard of evil. It is the peace which comes from those who communicate peace.

'They shall be called the sons of God' . . . Semitic languages are not rich in adjectives, but inventive in a metaphor which serves the same descriptive purpose. A writer might be 'a father of ink', a merciful God 'a father of mercies'. And so the utterly godlike might be called 'a son of God'. God is the supreme peacemaker, the great reconciler. His presence fuses dissidence in love, melts hostility. 'His words', said Ben Hur, tamed at last, 'took the sword out of my hand'. And Christ cannot penetrate His rebel world save in the lives and persons of His children, His peacemakers. And that is why, as Ruskin put it, 'no peace is in store for any of us, but that which we shall win by victory over shame and sin—victory over sin which oppresses as well as over that which corrupts'.

21 : The Persecuted

Matthew 5.10–12; John 16.1–6; Revelation 7.9–17

Here is a strange saying. The persecuted are numbered among the happy. It is not simply because of ultimate reward, when the wrongs of life are at last righted. It is because, in this world, the persecuted are commonly the good. In a corrupt society and a fallen world the spectacle of moral earnestness—such is human nature—offends the morally inert, and the sight of disciplined living rebukes and angers self-indulgence. The vested interests of vice fear virtue, and corruption is uneasy in the presence of a sterner and challenging uprightness.

A familiar pattern runs through all the history of man . . . 'Crucify him, away with him, not this man but Barabbas, he has a devil, a gluttonous man and a wine-bibber'. 'Then said Mr. No-good, "Away with such a fellow from the earth". "Ay", said Mr. Malice, "for I hate the very looks of him". Then said Mr. Love-lust, "I could never endure him". "Nor I", said Mr. Live-loose, "for he would ever be condemning my ways". "A sorry scrub", said Mr. High-mind . . . ' The smell of burning flesh, the reek of man's intolerance for man, fills history. Man will not have before his eyes the reproach of human goodness, if by stone, stick, or sword he can dash it from sight. And those sunnier generations which have imagined that such evil has at last been purged, have ended always like our own in sharp and rude awakening.

Professor Herbert Butterfield remarked in a significant passage: 'We are back for the first time in something like the earliest centuries of Christianity, and those centuries afford some relevant clues to the kind of attitude to adopt'.

No clear portrait of the persecuted emerges, as it does with the other Beatitudes. The persecuted are as varied as those who suffer for the Name. We met them in the Old Testament. We shall meet them in the New Testament. And there is persecution as subtle and as painful as that which tears body and limb. The coward's sneer, the cruel pressure of the conforming crowd, the uplifted academic eyebrow, the contempt of the corrupt 'inner ring'—all these make the way hard, lonely, sad for many good men and women, especially the young, who find ostracism more difficult to bear. Remember this in prayer and fellowship.

Questions and themes for study and discussion on Studies 14–21

1. What is 'hunger for righteousness'? Remember that those words were uttered in a hungry land.
2. Sorrow in God's plan. What did Rupert Brooke mean by the phrase: 'washed gloriously with sorrow'?
3. What is arrogance? Why does it preclude meekness?
4. Why is it impossible for the merciless to be Christian?
5. What does Paul mean by 'the peace . . . which passes all understanding' (Phil. 4.7)?
6. List forms of modern persecution.

RIGHTEOUSNESS IN CHRIST

Paul's Major Treatment of the Theme

22 : Righteousness Revealed

Romans 1.16–32

Paul is the great exponent of the theme of righteousness in Christ. In Romans he draws together the several strands of Old Testament teaching on this doctrine and sets them in the sharpened perspective of Christ's completed work. Yet Romans remains a missionary manifesto, written to encourage participation in Paul's mission to Spain (**1**.11 f.; **15**.17–24). The missionary character of the letter becomes clearer when the specific context for Paul's teaching concerning the righteousness of God is recognized. Paul speaks of righteousness or justification when discussing the relationship of Jews and Gentiles to each other and to the gospel (e.g. **1**.17 in the context of **1**.13–16, 18–32). His teaching on justification by faith is a pastoral response to a persistent question in the life of the early Church: how could the Jew and the Gentile stand on the same level of advantage before God? Paul demonstrates that at the point of plight there is no distinction between them. Both stand in urgent need of righteousness as an unconditional gift. God met their common need through Jesus Christ. The argument is doctrinally significant. Yet it remains intensely pastoral and practical. 'Justification by faith' is the keen statement of a missionary who reflected on the problem of sin and righteousness within the life of a church composed of Jews and Gentiles.

Paul's formulation of his theme in v. 16 is striking. This is a 'confessional' kind of affirmation related to Jesus' call for bold confession in a moment when the world asks you to be untrue to God (Mark **8**.38). Paul declares he is unashamed 'of Jesus and his words', which now means 'the gospel'. His commitment is supported by his experience of the power of God; through the gospel as he has preached it both Jews and Greeks have experienced God's saving righteousness. God's righteousness breaks through as the power by means of which He fulfils His will in the earth. He calls into existence a people who will honour Him as

God. This is what God has 'revealed' through the gospel, and the choice of the verb is significant for it always implies a certain hiddenness, and its unfolding with a certain surprise. From reflection on Hab. **2**.4 Paul understands that God's righteousness is appropriated on the ground of faith and leads to a life which finds its focus in faith in Christ.

There is another, more sobering aspect to the truth, however. The revelation of God's righteousness also entails the revelation of His wrath (18). God's wrath is His judging righteousness in response to the suppression of His truth. The doctrine of God's wrath safeguards the essential distinction between Creator and creature, which sin always seeks to minimize or erase. It is precisely within this context that the wrath of God is first introduced in Romans (21–23, 25, 28). The point of vs. 18–32 is that all men are guilty because they have rejected a knowledge of God which they possessed *and possess* (20). The mark of a godless world is not the ignorance of God, but rather the knowledge of God. That is why men are inexcusable and accountable to God (20; **2**.1). Without an appreciation of the severity of God's wrath we are unlikely to appreciate His provision of righteousness in Christ.

23 : The Gentiles and the Just Judgement of God

Romans 2.1–16

Paul's concern in Rom. **1**–**3** is to show the guilt of all men and their consequent need for the gift of righteousness in Christ. In **2**.1–16 the apostle adopts the form of dialogue and address to contrast human and divine judgement. He addresses himself first to man generally (1), and then specifically to the Gentiles (12–16). The key to this section is provided in v. 11: God is the impartial Judge. All of the several strands of the section confirm this truth and serve to vindicate the justice of God when He declares all men to be under the power of sin (**3**.9) and condemned in accordance with their works (6). The argument moves from the arrogance of sitting in judgement on others when we do what we condemn (1–3) to God's superlative kindness which can become the ground of human presumption (4, 5). The complete impartiality of the divine Judge is then affirmed by an elaborate parallelism (6–10). If it should be argued that the Gentiles cannot be held responsible by God because they did not know the Law, vs. 12–16 demonstrate that they *do* know and are therefore justly condemned. Within this structure v. 11 functions as a fulcrum on which the argument turns. Verses 1–10 build to v. 11 as their necessary conclusion, while vs. 12–16 develop the content and implications of v. 11.

Paul's treatment of the judgement according to works (6) and of Gentile responsibility (12–16) deserves consideration. The basis of the judgement of works is the fact that a man's character is displayed through his works. The last judgement does not determine if a man *is to be justified,* but only if in fact he *has been justified,* for in the final analysis his works can only declare his rebellion (cf. **3**.20). The man who is righteous through faith will also stand in this judgement, for faith *works* through love (Gal. **5**.6). The righteousness of God that becomes operative through faith produces obedience to God (cf. **13**.8–10; Gal. **5**.14). Thus the judgement of works will demonstrate the grace of God and His righteousness, as those works which issue from faith are manifested. Paul therefore implies the essential unity of faith and works in the context of a judgement that will demonstrate the failure of every human attempt at self-justification.

Verses 12–16 are addressed to the Gentiles who had no access to God's special revelation. Although the Law had not been revealed to them in the way it had been to the Jews, as created beings they possess certain universally valid norms of conduct which are part of God's revelation in creation. This means that they actually possess a certain knowledge of God within themselves. This argument is designed to show Gentile responsibility, for their moral faculty condemns their disobedience to the Law of God inherent in their created existence (**1**.32; **2**.1–3). Yet when Gentiles do what the Law requires, even though they do not possess the Mosaic Law, they become a shaming accusation against the more privileged Jews who do not obey what they clearly know to be God's revealed will.

Question: What will be the basis of your confidence as you reflect on your standing before the judgement of God?

24 : The Jews and the Just Judgement of God

Romans 2.17–29

Paul now turns his attention to the Jews whose possession of the Law supported their confidence that they enjoyed a special relationship to God (17). He begins by heaping up terms of praise (18–20), which in this context become an occasion, not for self-congratulation, but biting sarcasm. In normal usage the accumulated terms would have dignified Israel as the people called to be the teacher of the Gentile world. But in this context they are designed to shame Israel for its failure to observe the Law which was God's gift to the nation. The elaborate conditional construction ('But if . . . and if . . ., 17, 19) conveys an impression of emotional acceleration that suddenly shifts into a series of questions which drive home the argument (21–23). Each of the questions highlights an offence which the Jew would condemn, but each asks if he, in fact, is guilty of doing what he condemns. The implied response is clearly 'Yes'. The cumulative thought is that the one addressed, not only knows the Law, but teaches others, yet he performs actions which he seeks to prevent in others. The inevitable result is that God is dishonoured by the Gentiles (Isa. **52**.5). This impeachment is supported by enumerating the violations of the laws against stealing (21), adultery and idolatry (22) and blasphemy (23 f.). These items were included among those basic commandments which Jews of the first century believed were binding on all men. Purporting to be a guide to the blind (19), they proved to be blind themselves (cf. Matt. **15**.14).

The closely related issue of circumcision is treated in vs. 25–29. From a first-century Jewish perspective God's acceptance of men rested on their performance of the requirements of the Law and the covenant with Abraham (Gen. **15**), of which circumcision was the seal (Gen. **17**). Circumcision was regarded as effective precisely where the Law failed, since God was bound by His fidelity to keep the promise made to Abraham. Paul counters this false security with the painful truth that a Jew cannot take his stand as distinctive in circumcision unless he lives up to that Law of which circumcision is a witness (25). Moreover, the prescription of the Law possesses no power in itself to extend new life to men. What is required is that circumcision of the heart which God alone can achieve, so that the human will becomes synchronous with the divine will (29; cf. Deut. **10**.16; **30**.6; Jer. **4**.4; **9**.26). Apart from this action of God, the Jew, as much as the Gentile, stands condemned before God, lacking that righteousness which ensures justification.

Thought: *If one is performance-orientated, let his confidence be in the performance of Jesus Christ rather than in his own achievement.*

25 : The Righteousness of God Challenged

Romans 3.1–20

With this section the argument introduced in **1**.18 is brought to a forceful conclusion. These verses follow naturally on **2**.17–29 and are structurally related to that segment of the letter: reflection on the advantage of the Jew (**2**.17–20; **3**.1–4) leads to the recognition of the loss of that advantage (**2**.21–24; **3**.5–8) and its consequences (**2**.25–29; **3**.9–20). These considerations were crucial, for they demonstrate that all men, irrespective of their heritage, stand in need of God's provision of righteousness in Christ.

Paul had attacked in **2**.25–29 the false confidence of the Jew that, because of his circumcision, the mark of the Abrahamic covenant, God would exercise a double standard in the judgement favourable to him. He now locates the true advantage of the Jew in his possession of God's Word (1 f.). Judaism is rooted in the Old Testament with its promises, and the fulfilment of these promises is essential to the theme of God's righteousness. Paul has shown that the institutions of the old covenant, law and circumcision, are inadequate to shield the Jew from God's wrath. His confidence must rest therefore in another element of the covenant—the promise guaranteed by the fidelity of God (3 f.). Because God is inherently righteous, He will keep His promise. The citation of Psa. **51**.4 in v. 4 presupposes a judgement scene where God is both defendant and judge, for the vindication of God as righteous is set in the perspective of the last judgement. Although all men are unreliable, it will be established that God has fulfilled all His covenant obligations because He is reliable. Judaism's possession of the divine Word therefore demands the response of faith.

The irony exposed in vs. 5–8 is that man, confronted with his own unrighteousness, accuses God of being unrighteous (5, 7). Paul responds to this accusation by appealing to God's status as Judge of the world (6) and by demonstrating the unreasonableness to which false logic and human rationalization leads (8). In spite of the privileges enjoyed through the covenant, the Jew stands in danger of the divine wrath because he claims and applies those privileges wrongly. Basic to Paul's reply is the understanding of God's righteousness as His covenant faithfulness, which is to be the model for our own faithfulness.

Yet all men are unfaithful, and the conclusion that all men, both Jews and Gentiles, stand under the power and condemnation of sin (9) is supported by the strongest authority, by appeal to the Scriptures (10–18). The passages cited in this chain of references stress both individual and universal responsibility, and show that the whole sphere of human life is subject to sin and God's wrath. The fact that the whole world is finally reduced to silence before God (19 f.) demonstrates the inability of the Law to justify men and shield them from His retributive judgement. This exposure of the bankruptcy of the Law as the provider of life and vindication is the necessary preparation for the exposition of the new righteousness provided freely in Christ (**3**.21 ff.).

Thought: Those who know they will stand silent before God in the judgement learn now to be still and know that He is God.

26 : The Righteousness of God Vindicated

Romans 3.21–31

The significance of this passage to the theme of righteousness in Christ can scarcely be over-emphasized. It brings us to the heart of the gospel as do few other texts in the New Testament. Standing in sharp contrast to the long argument demonstrating that all men are sinners (**1**.18–**3**.20), it expounds the declarations of 1.16 f. and provides the bridge to the remaining sections of the letter. The recurring stress upon God's righteousness (21, 22, 24, 25, 26, 28, 30) together with the emphasis on faith (22, 25, 26, 27, 28, 30, 31) exposes the message of the entire epistle: God's righteousness . . . appropriated by faith.

Pointing to the radically new situation introduced by the cross of Christ, Paul declares solemnly and triumphantly that the righteousness of God to which Scripture bore eloquent witness has been manifested (21 f.). It was manifested historically in the complete obedience and death of Christ, whose faith and faithfulness motivated Him to comply fully with the will of the Father. Verse 22 develops the 'faith'-formula of 1.17 and would appear to speak of the faithfulness *of* Christ, not of faith *in* Christ (as in the RSV): Jesus' vicarious death in faithfulness to the divine intention results in the creation of the community of faith, those who believe in Jesus. Because salvation is achieved on the level of God's glory (rather than at the level of human achievement), it must be received by faith as the gift of God (23 f.). Incidentally, 'faith' and 'faithfulness' are two senses of the same Greek word.

Verses 24–26 clarify God's purpose in providing righteousness in Christ. He Himself is the author of the righteousness now available, for He has provided for propitiation which turned aside His wrath. The translation 'propitiation' is preferable to 'expiation' in v. 25. The means of propitiation is the blood of Christ. For this reason Jesus is the mediator of God's righteousness. His sacrificial death on the cross was the provision of God's invincible love, so that His love may achieve its purpose in a way that is entirely harmonious with the demands of His holiness (25 f.). His purpose, to make men righteous, demanded that He Himself should assume the initiative for the expiation of sin and rebellion. The proof that He has done so is the cross of Christ where God demonstrates that He is righteous. God makes men righteous because He is righteous. The only qualification is the requirement of faith on the part of the recipients of His action, and specifically, faith in Jesus as the mediator of the new righteousness.

The consequences of God's righteousness are momentous (27–31). (*i*) Justification is on the ground of faith in Jesus, because the principle of Law has been replaced by the principle of faith (27 f.). (*ii*) No room remains for boasting in human achievement. God's righteousness is established solely by His action and is imputed to men by the gracious disposition of God. (*iii*) God's provision is universal, covering the needs of both Jew and Gentile (29 f.). (*iv*) The Law is established in its basic design of bringing men into relationship with God, so that they will recognize God's good will for their lives and receive God's righteousness by grace (31). The driving force of Paul's language reveals the extent of his excitement in the achievement of God through Christ.

Question : When was the last time that the excitement of justification and righteousness as salvation breaking through really gripped you?

27 : Faith, Hope and the God who Raises the Dead

Romans 4

The consequences of God's disclosure of the new righteousness in Christ are so revolutionary that they need further explanation and proof from the Scriptures. This is provided in chapter **4** where Abraham and David serve as illustrations of what Paul has been saying. The apostle focuses on Gen. **15**.6 (3, 9, 22, 23) and Psa. **32**.1 (7, 8) to prove that justification has always been the free act of God appropriated through faith and not the performance of works. Abraham could assert no claim on righteousness. He came before God with empty hands and was justified for the sole reason that he believed in the divine promise (2–5). David's experience of forgiveness confirms that pardon is extended to the man who has only his sins to offer to God (6–8). Man has no valid work to show God that can attract His favour; his sins are not balanced by his merits. They are simply forgiven by God who startles men with His grace. What Abraham and David shared in common was their faith in God's promise, which brought into operation justification and pardon.

The consideration of Abraham's circumcision in vs. 9–15 sharpens the issue. Circumcision was the sign, but not the cause, of God's gift of righteousness; it was a seal, confirming a righteousness which had already been given to him.

The works of a believer, like Abraham's circumcision, are his response to the experience of divine grace, and play no part in the securing of justification (11 f.). This fact indicates that it was God's purpose to establish in history an 'economy' of grace. His design was to make Abraham the father of a people who exercise the same faith he had exercised when he believed the promise of God (16 f.). The radical nature of Abraham's faith is underscored: the fulfilment of the promise was as impossible as raising the dead (17, 19). From a human perspective, Abraham was the prisoner of his past. Yet the promise was to Abraham as good as fulfilment, for he had an unwavering confidence in God's sovereign will (20 f.). His faith was the assurance that God, not his past, determined the future. The future would be new since God had declared He was about to intervene and do something new. The faith that is 'reckoned for righteousness' (22) is thus radiant with hope because it is focused on the future and rests in God.

While this long discourse centres on Abraham, Paul's concern is with every believer in all ages (23–25). What is said of Abraham is valid for us. The God in whom Abraham believed, who makes the dead to live, is also the God of our faith who raised Jesus Christ from the dead (17, 24). Like Abraham, we are justified by faith in the God of the promise. For us the promise is disclosed and fully present in the resurrection of Christ. What the believer is to learn from 'the father of the faithful' is to resign every attempt to create a righteousness of his own and to abandon himself to the working of God.

28 : Righteousness Based on Faith

Romans 10.1–13

Paul genuinely loved his own people (1). The realization that the Gentiles were receiving righteousness through faith while Israel blindly continued to attempt to establish its own righteousness on the ground of performance (**9**.30–33) greatly saddened him. He freely acknowledges the zeal for God found in Judaism (2, cf. Gal. **1**.13 f.; Phil. **3**.6), but it was a zeal uninformed by the knowledge of God's achievement in Christ (**3**.21–26). The failure to submit to the righteous action of God reduced the Jews to pursuing their own righteousness through Law-observance. It reflected ignorance of the fact that nothing short of God's righteousness will satisfy God's requirement (2 f.). Submission to God leads to dependence on God and the repudiation of all self-dependence. The Law was never intended to be a means to the attainment of righteousness. Its function was to provoke responsibility toward God by highlighting the need for a righteousness that only God could confer. The meaning of v. 4, accordingly, is that Christ is 'the goal' to which the Law pointed (cf. Gal. **3**.24). Paul does not have in mind an old way that came to an end (righteousness through obedience to the Law), but a false way that ends (the attempt to justify oneself through works) because the One to whom the Law bore witness (cf. **3**.21) has come and has perfectly fulfilled its claims by His obedience. On the ground of *His* achievement God may bestow righteousness on those who trust in Him.

This is made clearer in vs. 5–13 where Paul brings together Lev. **18**.5 and Deut. **30**.11–14 to show that Moses understood that grace would be required for Israel to experience life with God. The detail that the word is 'on your lips and in your heart' (8) indicates that the inwardness of God's working is in view. The attempt to make salvation dependent on human achievement obscures this essential insight. Man can do nothing. He can neither bring the Messiah down from God's presence nor raise Him from the dead (6–8), for in fact He has already come down and has already been raised up. This means that salvation is accomplished by God's power alone. We must stop trying to do something to merit salvation and must believe and receive the accomplished redemption in Christ. Paul therefore calls for a vital, confessing faith in Jesus as Lord and in God who by His power raised Jesus from the dead (9 f.). Paul sees no essential difference between *personal faith* in Jesus as Lord and propositional faith in the fact that God raised Him from the dead. The Christ we trust *is* the One who was raised from death. The prophetic witness of Isa. **28**.16 is added to the earlier citations from the Law (5–8, 11) to confirm that the way of obtaining righteousness has always been the way of faith. This is valid for all men, for Jew as well as Gentile, since Jesus is Lord of all and is ready to bestow the benefits of His death on all who trust in Him (12 f.). Righteousness is located solely in Christ.

Thought : Since salvation is God's achievement, the goal of human life must be the enjoyment of God for ever.

Questions and themes for study and discussion on Studies 22–28

1. Is a reticence to share our Christian faith with others evidence that we are ashamed of the gospel? How can we become more confident in our ability to commend the gospel to others? How will we explain to them the concept of righteousness?
2. Three times Paul speaks of God giving men over to self-destruction and evil behaviour (Rom. **1**.24, 26, 28). Is this reflected in the contemporary concern for liberalization of laws governing abortion, homosexuality and related matters? What considerations will contribute to a Christian attitude toward such questions?
3. Does Rom. **2**.14–16 have any bearing on the missionary mandate to disciple all nations? Is there any suggestion in this passage that one could find a righteous person who would not require evangelization?
4. Possession of the Law gave to the Jews of Paul's day a false sense of security which kept them from recognizing their need for righteousness in Christ. What factors hinder men today?
5. Read Rom. **3**.21–26 in several contemporary translations, noting the variety of ways in which the vocabulary of righteousness and justification is rendered. Compose your own version of this crucial passage, so that a child, a teenager person, the 'man in the street' can understand what Paul is saying.

CHARACTER STUDIES

29 : The Salt of the Earth

Matthew 5.13–16; Genesis 18.16–33

The crowd sat among the wild flowers on the hill above the lake. They listened entranced as the characters of the Kingdom rose and walked before them, stirring hunger, calling to the heart, eliciting desire . . .

In a sudden turn of speech, commencing at v. 11, Christ changed from the third person to the second, 'You', He said, 'are the salt of the earth' (13). And so we meet the Remnant again, the happy few, 'those who feared the Lord' of Mal. 3.16. Salt is a vivid figure. Salt gives savour, and Christians should provide the tang and challenge of life. Salt preserves from corruption. It is ludicrous to imagine that Christian values, and therefore the virtues which cement society, and the Christian ethics without which a nation crumbles, can survive the creed which formed and fed them, or those who held the creed.

Remove 'the salt of the earth' and corruption is inevitable. There comes the recognizable condition of Alfred's prophecy in Chesterton's poem:

. . . thought a crawling ruin,
. . . life a leaping mire,
. . . a broken heart in the breast of the world,
And the end of the world's desire.

That is why every evil force which society spawns is eager, as we saw when we looked at the persecuted of the earth, to dash Christians aside. They remind the world of better things, visible as the medieval cities which the Mediterranean world can show, set high for safety on some steep eminence, at the end of a climbing road. Or like the flame of a lamp, small perhaps, but until doused and stifled, visible from uncannily far away. We quoted Portia on mercy. She also said to Nerissa in that same play:

How far that little candle throws its beams!
So shines a good deed in a naughty world.

An 'evil world', Shakespeare meant. 'Naughty' is one of those words which evil has eroded.

But a last thought for those who are 'the salt of the earth', that group to which the one who writes here on this winter's night, and you who read, are called to belong. Salt, said a Chinese girl, makes one thirsty. Do we make those around us thirst for righteousness, for the water of life, for that which has obviously quenched our restless thirst? Do we?

30 : Children of the Father

Matthew 5.17–48; John 10.1–13

In Matt. **5** let us look especially at the last six verses with their cameo picture of the Christian. The Lord has spoken much of the claims, beyond the claims of the Law, which He made on the life committed to Him, and He is still on that theme.

Verse 43 touched a common Jewish heresy. 'Revenge is the Jew's right,' says old Simonides in *Ben Hur,* 'it is the Law. A camel, yes, even a dog, remembers the wrong done to it.' Many a page of history between the Testaments bears witness to that belief. And here is a curious fact. A large number of the people gathered before Him on the hillside when Christ preached His sermon were, in fact, folk who 'hungered and thirsted after righteousness'. They were 'hungry sheep who looked up and were not fed', betrayed and starved by the false shepherds.

They had gone out into the wilderness to hear the fervent preacher who was the forerunner of Christ. And like John they must have known of the desert ascetics, one of whose places of retreat was at Qumran. Among the Dead Sea Scrolls, the surviving library of the Qumran community, there is a strange allegorical document called 'The War of the Children of Light and the Children of Darkness.' It is a curious compilation, a sort of pious guerrilla manual, built out of what appears to have been a Roman military text-book, and a study of the wars of the Old Testament.

Perhaps it was knowledge of such teaching which convinced the Romans in A.D. 68 that the place was a nest of terrorists and partisans, and led to the destruction of the site. But Christ and His hearers may also have heard of the book, for the book exhorts: 'Love the Children of Light, and hate the Children of Darkness.'

The Children of the Father (45), the Salt of the Earth (13), the Light of the World (14), are not of this dark pattern.

As Phillips puts it in his apt rendering of John 1.16, there is 'grace in our lives because of His grace'. The Children of the Father, as the last challenging verse puts it, move towards the likeness of their parent. It is, in the original text, more of a future statement than a command. It touches the same truth as that other word which assures us that 'we shall be like Him, because we shall see Him as He is' (1 John 3.2).

31 : The Hypocrite

Matthew 6.1–4; 23.13–36

Among the characters who walked before the hearers on the hillside was a sinister person clothed to deceive. He pretended to be one of them, but merely played a part. He was an actor and the word hypocrite means precisely that.

That hypocrisy should be practised under the scorn of all the centuries is a matter of astonishment. The theme has exercised the rhetoric of all the past, for among the characters of Scripture there is none who so universally wins disapproval, even, at times, when the disapproval itself is a species of hypocrisy.

Said Francis Bacon: 'A bad man is worse when he pretends to be a saint.' 'Satan,' said Milton, 'was the first to practise falsehood under a saintly show.' 'Hypocrisy is the homage which vice pays to virtue', said the cynical Rochefoucauld. Said Pope: 'A hypocrite makes a sombre jest of God and religion.' And Johnson, echoing the Frenchman: 'The hypocrite shows the excellence of virtue by the necessity he feels himself under of seeming to be virtuous.'

In v. 2 there is an interesting word. When translating 'have' from the Lord's Aramaic into Greek, Matthew used a compound verb. The commercial meaning of this word was unknown until the discovery of masses of receipted bills among the Greek papyri from Egypt. The form of receipt was the phrase 'he is quit', and the verb used in Matthew for, 'they have their reward', is this very verb. Matthew the tax collector, the underling of the Roman tax-gathering machine, had doubtless written this word on settled tax-accounts more frequently than any other word that had ever come from his reed pen. And now, in a flash of satire, he sees the hypocrite, courting popular awe and wonderment by overdone and pompous public acts of piety. He thinks of his receipts, and as he translates the prose from the Sermon he slips a commercial reference in for vividness—'In truth they are quit, their full reward is paid.' God, as it were, no man's debtor, pays them spot cash, in the debased currency which their sinful souls covet. They get their meed of empty adulation, and Heaven is free of its obligations.

And so with Matthew we bow the hypocrite out. He will come back again, for nothing daunts him. He never learns his lesson.

32 : The Man of Prayer

Matthew 6.5–7; 1 Kings 18.25–41

The man of prayer is a sincere man. He makes no hypocritical stance. He seeks privacy with God. The 'closet' of the AV (KJV) is as colourless as the 'room' of RSV. A 'tameion' or 'tamieion' was a storeroom, some 'lean-to' on the cool side of the house, where a peasant or fisherman stored his dried fish and fruit, the only place of privacy in the homes of poor Galileans.

The man of prayer is an honest man, never more penetratingly honest with himself, never more ruthless in self-examination, never more ready to see himself as he is seen, than when he seeks God in prayer. The Lord has just spoken of the false face with which hypocrites deceive the world, but how can a man wear cover or disguise before his God? The soul is naked in His presence. At prayer's beginning a man must have done with lying, deception, excuses, posing, play-acting in all its forms.

The man of prayer is a man of faith. He does not think of God as the dervish priests of Baal thought of him, with their day-long chant and sanguinary mutilations; nor as the Ephesian mob thought of their city's patron goddess, intoning for two long hours: 'Great is Artemis of Ephesus.' A man's prayers are not only the measure of his Christianity, they reveal his understanding of God. That is why prayer is the place of testing, for prayer is itself a challenge to doubt and to all material and carnal preoccupation.

That is why prayer can at times be the place of conflict. The place of prayer bears that very name in the exquisite Blue Mosque at Istanbul. The nooks where private prayer is made are called 'the Battleground', for the Moslem, in this sphere, has glimpsed the truth that prayer is a confrontation with evil, and no man has won a deep and vital knowledge of prayer who has not been at grips with the powers of darkness. 'O the pure delight of a single hour that before Thy throne I spend', runs an old hymn. Before such serenity is won, many a solitary conflict has been battled through.

Prayer is communion and communication with God. 'Oh, that I knew where I might find him,' cried Job (**23**.3), and effectively to pray is an art which must be learned. The things of time and place, the world and the flesh press in, and prayer tails off in incoherence and preoccupation. That is why the man of prayer is a man who has cared enough to learn to pray (Luke **11**.1).

33 : Child of the Father

Matthew 6.9–7.6; Acts 17. 23–29; Luke 11.1–4

In fifty-seven words, excluding the doxology at the end, the Lord taught His disciples how to pray. The man of prayer is truly a 'son of the Father' (Matt. **5**.44 f.), because the prayer begins with an acknowledgement of that relationship. The challenge stands like a sentinel at the opening. He who utters the words: 'Our Father . . .' must pause in gratitude, worship and self-examination. The fatherhood of God is an amazing concept. The Old Testament sometimes used the idea of parental love as an illustration of the love of God. Enlightened pagans, like the Stoic poet whom Paul quoted in his address to the Athenian philosophers, had deduced from the creative act of God a notion of divine fatherhood for all the race. But only in Christ is the truth seen in full fruit and power.

Who 'in Christ' may call God 'Father'? Not simply those who are conscious of their Creator. The charter of our sonship is John **1**.12. It is well, then, if we use the phrases of this prayer as the rosary of our devotions, to pause on the threshold and give thanks for the gift of grace, and the price that was paid, while in the same surge of gratitude we reaffirm the faith that laid strong hold on it.

To a loving father access is immediate and unquestioned for any child. There is no closed door between, no barriers of ritual or human mediation. If God is 'our Father', He is near, ready to hearken, eager to receive. When a Christian has uttered the opening words of the prayer, he has expressed the ultimate experience a human being can have of God. Here is the very substance of our religion, the concept that infuses all Christian theology.

But such a Father! Let us not build Him on 'false notions of our own' (Psa. **50**.21). He is no Roman *paterfamilias,* no 'Mr. Barrett of Wimpole Street', 'coming in terror like the King of kings' . . . But on the other hand He is no weakling, culpably indulgent and ready to spoil in love's name . . . But this 'character' risks becoming a description of God, not man. We are still with the Man of Prayer, and see him now in the place of adoration in which he finds refreshment, washing, sanctification. He knows the Father's presence is his right in Christ, but he does not burst into that holy place petulantly, unprepared, brashly and presumptuously. He enters and bows low.

34 : The Steadfast Petitioner

Matthew 7.7–23; Luke 11.5–13; Genesis 32.24–28

The man of prayer is a man of quiet and steadfast faith. The threefold command of Matt. **7**.7 sets this forth. No frivolous asking, no wrong search, no arrogant knocking on the door, is envisaged. The picture is that of a suppliant approaching a gracious superior, an earnest seeker after truth and righteousness, a friend or member of a family coming home.

Note secondly, the rising earnestness in 'ask', 'seek' and 'knock'. The last presupposes confidence in present ability to answer. And thirdly, note that the imperatives, like the participles which parallel them in the next verse, are couched in the present tense. This tense in Greek implies continuity. It is a 'linear' tense, and it would not be wrong to translate: 'Keep on asking . . . keep on seeking . . . keep on knocking, for the one who keeps on asking receives, and the one who keeps on seeking finds, and to the one who keeps on knocking, the door shall be opened.' The notion of persistence is much sharper in the Greek text than in the English translations.

God's delays are purposeful, His plans are above our plans, and His thoughts above our thoughts, 'as the heavens are higher than the earth'; and in delay He tests our earnestness, cleanses our motives, reshapes our petition and brings it into conformity with His will. He does 'exceeding abundantly above all we ask or think', but often effects this blessing by the very process of delay.

There is no trickery or guile in His answer. Mythology has more than one tale to tell of the treachery of pagan deities. Tithonus prayed for immortality, and it was granted him. He forgot to pray for eternal youth, and so for ever grew older. Semele prayed that she might look on Zeus, and was incinerated in the answer to her prayer. Midas prayed that what he touched might turn to gold, and found his food turn metal on his tongue. God is not thus. He answers and 'adds no sorrow'.

Hence the simple words of vs. 9 and 10. There is a superficial resemblance between a stone and a loaf. In the desert, hungering after His fast, the Lord had pictured the reality of bread in the mocking stones at His feet. Hence, perhaps, this parallel. A snake and a fish have similar resemblance, and likewise an egg and the round, hard-shelled, crab-like scorpion of Palestine. God does not deal thus cynically with His children. 'Good things' are His promise, and if man seeks to give good gifts to those whom he imperfectly loves, how much more will Perfect Love and Perfect Wisdom grant blessing to His Children.

35 : The Two Builders

Matthew 7.24–27; 1 Corinthians 3.9–23

The two men who close the Sermon on the Mount might be any one of us. The word used in the Greek text for 'rock' is 'petra', which means a 'crag', some great outcrop of the earth's solidity. In the Lord's picture it probably indicates the rock walls of some river-valley, and the man who builds on it has his house high and firm, founded with the flat valley-floor of what the Arabs call a 'wadi' beneath him.

For most of the year the valley floor is dry and empty, but when some storm-born freshet in the distant watershed fills it fathoms deep with rushing water, that man's house is safe which stands on the living rock. The second man has chosen the sandy levels below on the floor of the wadi. It is far easier to build there. Furthermore, the valleys between their stony cliffs are the highways to the interior. The caravans pass that way. Trade goes with the caravans, and the faces of men are seen on the easy highway of the valley bottom. The man who seeks the day's quick advantage naturally chooses that place for his habitation. It is not lonely, not conspicuous, but popular, and certainly cheaper and better for business to site one's home where the multitude go by.

To build on the crag is frequently derided, it makes sometimes for loneliness, it is conspicuous because it is different. So it often is with the man who chooses the foundation 'other than that which no man can lay' (1 Cor. 3.11). And all seems well with the hard-headed fellow who knows where worldly advantage lies until there comes the day of stress and testing. 'The day will reveal it,' says Paul, and there is sometimes a judgement before the Judgement Day which tries the foundation on which men build the foundation of their lives.

Perhaps these men are the two best known characters of all time. They comprise, each in his own way, the two great divisions of humanity. The rock is one, the sand of varied composition. The floods are of one kind and another, but the end is the same . . .

We come unto our fathers' God:
Their Rock is our salvation:
The Eternal Arms, their dear abode,
We make our habitation:
Safe in the same dear dwelling-place,
Rich with the same eternal grace,
Bless the same boundless Giver!

(Thomas Hornblower Gill)

Questions and themes for study and discussion on Studies 29–35

1. How has Christianity created Western civilization?
2. Why must the collapse of faith in a sufficiently large group corrupt a society?
3. The Fatherhood of God as a Christian doctrine.
4. How is hypocrisy avoided?
5. How does prayer test sincerity, faith and honesty?
6. What of the place of prayer? Consider prayer in the lives of three Old Testament characters.
7. How does persistence test and deepen prayer?
8. What does the sand of the Parable of the Builders represent in modern life?

RIGHTEOUSNESS IN CHRIST

Justification Elsewhere in the New Testament

36 : Humility and Justification

Luke 18.9–17

It is characteristic of men to compare themselves favourably with other men. This was as true in the first century as it is in the twentieth, and Jesus had to deal with this attitude in the Pharisees (9). His parable presents two men and their attitudes, and discloses God's response to them. The disturbing, revolutionary character of Jesus' teaching will be appreciated when it is remembered that the populace viewed a Pharisee as pious, just and honourable, while a tax collector was regarded as a grafter and a scoundrel, an outcast from society. In the interpretation of the parable we must not blacken the Pharisee and dissociate him from ourselves. He recognized God's Temple as a house of prayer (10). What Jesus condemned was his basic attitude of heart and mind. He was aware of particular sins (11), but not of his position as a sinner in the presence of a holy God. He knew sin only as gross sin, but not as hostility toward God or the lifting up of oneself in pride before God. He was therefore comfortable in placing himself in a category distinct from others, and displayed arrogance toward God. When he spoke of his piety (12), it was not the practice of fasting or tithing that Jesus condemned but his attitude of boasting: he had done more than the Law required and God had to be reminded of his excessive merit. Because his piety had become an end in itself it had become abortive. The excess is not wrong, for God is worthy of all of our strength and possessions, but boasting before God is abhorrent.

By contrast, there was a genuine sense of awe and reverence before God in the tax collector as he approached Him in prayer. He sensed the distance between himself as sinner and God as pure holiness. His spirit was deeply agitated in his consciousness of being in the presence of God (13). His prayer displays the attitude which God approves. It should be translated literally, 'Be propitious to me, *the* sinner.' The only sinner the tax collector knows about in

God's presence is himself (contrast v. 11). His prayer for propitiation reflects an awareness of God's wrath on sin, and the fervent desire that God should intervene to turn that wrath aside. The tax collector concentrated his prayer on his deepest need; his status as a sinner who could receive righteousness only as God's gracious action. Jesus' statement that he went to his home 'justified' (14) underscores the humility before God which is appropriate to us all in our need for God's righteousness. What is demanded is the disposition of children who take openly and confidently what is given to them (15–17). Unlike adults, who do not want anything given to them, children are comparatively modest and unspoiled. The kingdom belongs to such as these because they receive it as a gift. The ground of Jesus' surprising statement is not to be found solely in any subjective quality possessed by children but rather in their humble condition and in the startling character of the grace of God who wills to give the kingdom, and righteousness, to those who have no claim upon it.

Thought: *The demand that a man become as a little child calls for a fresh realization that he is utterly helpless in his relationship to the kingdom of God. The kingdom, like righteousness, is what God gives and a man receives.*

37 : The Quest for Eternal Life

Luke 18.18–30

The utter impossibility of justifying ourselves before God through anything we do is underscored in the account of a wealthy ruler who consulted Jesus about inheriting eternal life (18–27). The form of his question, '*What shall I do . . . ?*' (18) implies a piety of achievement which stands in contrast to Jesus' teaching that a man must *receive* life as a gift from God in his helplessness (17). In the light of vs. 20 f., the ruler evidently thought there were conditions to be fulfilled beyond those set out in the Law. Jesus' response to the title of respect, 'Good Teacher' (18 f.) served to sharpen the issue. The inquirer's idea of goodness was defined by human achievement. He undoubtedly regarded himself as 'good' since he was confident that he had fulfilled the commandments from the time he first assumed their yoke as a very young man (21). Jesus' response that only God is good (19) forces him to recognize that his only hope is an utter reliance on God who alone can grant eternal life (27). The appeal to the commandments (20) serves to reinforce this truth: Jesus does not accept as good any other will than the will of God revealed in the Law.

When the man replied impulsively that he had fulfilled the Law's demand Jesus called him to that self-sacrificing devotion which characterizes every true follower of Jesus (22). Keeping the individual commandments is no substitute for the readiness for self-surrender to the absolute claim of God. Self-surrender implies a renunciation of all achievement and the reception of righteousness and life as a man who possesses nothing. In the case of the wealthy ruler, his reduction to poverty and helplessness would dramatize the fact that man is helpless in his quest for eternal life, which must be bestowed as the gift of God. His tragic decision to reject Jesus' call to discipleship reflects a greater love for his possessions than for life (23). In his case the Law had not yet fulfilled its function, for its task is to bring man's satisfaction with this world to an end and to quicken within him a thirst for righteousness and life. Jesus' comment in v. 24 calls attention to the peculiar danger confronting the rich because of the false sense of security which wealth creates. Both the Law and the gospel demand a whole-hearted reliance on God (24–27).

In contrast to the wealthy ruler, the disciples had abandoned everything in order to follow Jesus (28). There appears to be a note of self-congratulation in this declaration. It reflects a tendency to think of the rewards of service before the nature of the mission has been understood. Nevertheless, Peter's words show that he has understood Jesus' mandate in the absolute sense it bears in v. 22. Jesus' reply indicates that God takes nothing away from a man without restoring it to him in a new and glorious form (29 f.). The promise of eternal life in the age to come echoes the concern of the wealthy ruler and looks beyond the loss sustained through allegiance to God to the triumph assured to those who receive life as God's justifying action.

Thought: *Behind a façade of security there may dwell a heart that has lost much of its security. Ultimate security rests in utter reliance on God alone.*

38 : Pardon or Peril

Acts 13.36–52

In Antioch of Pisidia Paul addressed the synagogue congregation consisting of resident Jews and converts from the local population (14-43). His recital of redemptive history rapidly reviews God's activity from the Exodus to the ministry of the Baptist (17–25) as the prelude to the presentation of the death and resurrection of Jesus (26–35). Paul concentrates on Jesus' resurrection (30–37) because that historical fact indicates that God has acted decisively to save His people, fulfilling the hope of Israel (22 f., 26, 32 f., 41). What determines whether men experience pardon or rejection is the response to Jesus Himself (38–41).

Within this framework Paul speaks of sin and righteousness (38 f.). While the Mosaic Law had been able to expose sin, it was powerless to set men free from enslavement to sin. Moreover, the Law could never justify anyone from anything, for all have transgressed it. While provision was made for atonement from sins committed in ignorance, there was no provision for sins committed 'with a high hand', in deliberate rebellion against God. The Mosaic Law prescribed the full penalty. The promise of justification from all sins and complete acceptance before God which is extended to those who place their faith in Jesus derives from the fact that He bore the penalty of sin and was vindicated as righteous by His resurrection. Jesus' resurrection thus creates both a new invitation to trust in God's saving activity (as reviewed in vs. 17–25) and poses a new peril for those who remain obstinately in an unbelief condemned by Scripture (Hab. **1**.5 cited in v. 41). What is demanded is steadfast reliance on the grace of God (43).

The excited response of the Gentile population to this message a week later stirred up bitter opposition to Paul's preaching (44 f.). The majority of the Jews undoubtedly regarded his offer of a right relationship with God on the ground of faith in Jesus alone as a violation of God's covenant of circumcision. They refused to believe in Jesus and may have spoken derogatorily of Him when they reviled Paul. The apostle recognized in their hostile reaction the fulfilment of prophecy (Isa. **49**.6) and the mandate to offer the gospel directly to the Gentiles (46–47). Israel's blindness would prevent them from fulfilling their world-mission of bearing light to the Gentiles. The significant response of faith on the part of the local populace validated Paul's message, while the qualification that 'as many as were ordained to eternal life believed' (48) affirms that the bestowal of righteousness remains God's sovereign prerogative. When Paul and his party were expelled from the city they 'shook off the dust from their feet' (51). This was a symbolic gesture that they dissociated themselves from a people whose repudiation of the good news of righteousness in Christ invited the judgement of God.

Question: *If the 'No' of the Jew permitted the free offer of the gospel to the Gentile, what is the responsibility of the Gentile Christian to the unbelieving Jew?*

39 : The Collapse of Self-confidence

Philippians 3.1–11

Paul's harsh words in v. 2 are directed against certain Judaizers who attempted to make submission to the Law and circumcision a prerequisite for salvation. He brands their activity as 'mutilation of the flesh', contrary to the Roman laws governing the colony of Philippi (cf. Acts **16**.21). Gentile Christians actually constitute the true circumcision which God approves (cf. Deut. **10**.16), since they have renounced all claim to merit and base their confidence on God alone (3). Paul shows that from a human point of view he possessed both inherited and acquired advantages of which he might boast, among which he lists circumcision, earnest piety and fanatical zeal. His strict observance of the Law would have won a verdict of 'blameless' in any human court (4–6). But if Paul had once drawn support from these facts for his relationship to God, he now categorizes them as 'loss' (7), because they encouraged a false sense of security and dulled his sensitivity to God's indictment of his *goodness* (cf. Isa. **64**.6). As such, they constituted an impediment that stood in the way of his coming to faith in Christ. Every Christian who reflects on his former attitudes and conduct is forced to recognize this for the sake of Christ. How do you view your own 'virtues'?

What altered Paul's perspective was the irresistible intervention of the risen Lord in his life. From that moment the fanatical persecutor of the Church (6) became the devoted disciple of Jesus Christ who now acknowledges that the one treasure worth possessing is the knowledge of Christ (8–10). The knowledge to which Paul refers is not simply intellectual but personal, intimate and practical. It flows from the vital union of the believer with Christ, so that the life of Christ is mediated to the Christian through the Holy Spirit. Paul stresses two consequences which flow from his union with Christ. (*i*) One who knows Jesus in this way has abandoned all efforts to establish his own righteousness or *to achieve* the status of 'blamelessness' (cf. v. 6). He is content *to receive* a righteousness which God gives only to the person who has surrendered to God's judgement on his 'goodness' (9). This collapse of self-confidence is the essence of faith from a human point of view; it is an expression of confidence in the achievement of Jesus Christ alone. (*ii*) The intense desire to know Christ which flows from this union demands an identification with Christ in His resurrection and sufferings (10). We are to experience the power of His resurrection in order to be enabled to participate in the sufferings which were Christ's (cf. 2 Cor. **4**.10–14). Paradoxically, this preparation for sharing the experience of Christ's death, which is achieved through the appropriation of the power of His resurrection, leads full circle back to the experience of resurrection power itself (11). The righteousness experienced through vital union with Christ thus moulds a man's character even as it assures him of full acceptance with God.

Question: *Has your knowledge of Christ matured since you first came to faith in Him?*

40 : Faith Validated by Works

James 2.14–26

It is common to set this section, with its stress on works, in opposition to the Pauline teaching that justification is by faith alone. This, however, is to misunderstand the intention of James. His concern is not to challenge Paul's teaching but to underscore the necessity for a vital, active faith that significantly affects the way a man thinks and acts. Paul would thoroughly support James' contention that a faith which fails to find practical expression in human relationships is a hollow mockery of the faith God approves (cf. Eph. **2**.8–10; Tit. **1**.16; **3**.7 f.). Authentic faith will always issue in a life-style that will commend itself to other men. To illustrate his point James describes a situation of gross insensitivity to acute human need (15 f.). The dismissal of shivering, starving members of the church with an empty wish that their needs may be met, when what is required is food and clothing, betrays a callousness of spirit that springs from an unregenerate heart. James may be remembering actual conditions in Jerusalem (cf. Acts **11**.28–30). If your 'faith' contents itself with pious phrases in the face of dire need, it is 'dead' because it is void of power (17). It can neither justify nor save. It can only offend, placing obstacles in the path of others who need to come to authentic faith.

The intimate relationship of faith and works is clarified in vs. 18–26. James' point is that faith becomes visible in the sphere of human affairs only as it is put into action. The confession that God is one (19, cf. Deut. **6**.4) was cherished by Judaism and Christianity (cf. Mark **12**.29 f.; 1 Cor. **8**.6). Confession, however, that lacks validation in life puts man in the same category as the demonic powers who shudder in anticipation of the sentence of judgement from God (19). The doctrine that faith must be accompanied by works which prove to men its vital quality is illustrated by reference to Abraham and Rahab (20–25). James, like Paul, knows that Abraham was justified *before God* by faith, for he cites Gen. **15**.6 in v. 23. He introduces the offering of Isaac (Gen. **22**), however, as evidence that the patriarch was 'justified by works'. This statement means that he was justified by works *before men* as he demonstrated the integrity of his confidence in God. His works 'justified' or validated the genuineness of his faith in God. Rahab, similarly, demonstrated through the kindness extended to Joshua and Caleb that she really trusted in the God of Israel. Faith must issue in responsible action that commends the godly quality of faith to others.

Thought: *No man is justified by faith unless faith has made him just.*

Questions and themes for study and discussion on Studies 36–40

1. What evidence is there in contemporary society that God

is actively bringing outcasts in society to an experience of justification?

2. What can be done by the Church to confront the wealthy with their need of righteousness in Christ?
3. Does Jesus commend poverty as a life-style for all men? Is there a virtue in being poor that attracts the favourable attention of God?
4. Does the promise of justification through faith in Jesus (e.g. Acts **13**.38 f.) encourage an attitude of moral laxity? What is the dynamic for moral rectitude that God's righteousness introduces in the lives of men?
5. What implications for Christian social action may be derived from James' insistence on the validation of faith through works?

CHARACTER STUDIES

41 : Herod

Mark 6.14–29; John 3.19–36

Herod stands full length in these verses. A guilty conscience never feels safe. An evil deed had a witness in the wretched king's heart, and by his own cowardice he had produced the little hell in which he lived; for Herod had been touched by John's preaching (20). The words may be rendered: 'Herod respected John. He knew that he was a just, good man, and paid attention to him. He listened willingly to John's preaching, and John's words deeply influenced his conduct.' A surprising statement, a moving picture of what might have been. The bad blood of the old Idumaean murderer of children ran in his veins, but no one is beyond God's grace or the touch of His Holy Spirit, and a longing for purity had briefly stirred in Herod's heart. Too weak to act upon it and to do justice to his wronged wife who had fled to her father in Petra, too firmly bound by the fascination of a corrupt woman to break free, the king delayed, and found himself betrayed into deeper crime. Playing the great man in his fortress banqueting-hall, Herod joined in the cheering at Salome's lascivious dance, and made his reckless promise. The price of freedom grows with each hesitation to claim it, and Herod was faced with a dilemma. 'By and by'—this phrase in the AV (KJV) of v. 25 is incorrect. The RSV is correct with the phrase 'at once'. Salome knew her victim, and asked for John's head 'immediately', on a plate. Herod bought that one moment's prestige with years of mental torment. There is no treasure like a clean conscience. If conscience is stained, clean it by confession, and set it beneath the Cross.

Conscience, Herod's tormentor, had once been his friend. Conscience can be the point of impact of God's Spirit on the mind. Relentlessly, God pursues the soul of man, presses hard upon his sin, and stirs a restlessness which can find assuagement only in surrender. A man is only finally lost when God ceases to press upon him. The moment may sometimes be observed. Such a crisis came when the Lord looked at Judas and said in flat dull tones: 'What you are going to do, do quickly'. Judas went out, and, says John, 'It was night'. At the Machaerus party, Herod stepped into the dark.

42 : Herodias

Matthew 14.1–14; Galatians 6.7–8

It could have been somewhere before A.D. 23 that Herod Antipas met his brother Philip's wife in Rome. This Philip was not Herod's fellow-tetrach, but another member of the family, who lived quietly in the capital, too quietly for his restless dynamic wife, who had all of the Herodian love of action and intrigue. When Herod appeared, she saw, like Bathsheba, the chance of a royal alliance, and rescue from her boredom. She set out to win him—no very difficult task. Such women bend the carnal, the sensual and the weak easily to their will. Herod no doubt knew the brief sense of victory and exhilaration sensed by fools when they have won cheap pleasure, and the bill in terms of pain, shame and disillusionment is not yet presented for payment.

Herodias was determined to be queen, no mere paramour, and the shameless couple set out for Palestine. Herod's many foes, or her own spies, soon informed Herod's legitimate wife, fiery daughter of the ruler of the proud Nabataeans, the Arabian tribe whose rock-cut capital of Petra, 'the rose-red city, half as old as time', lay in the eastern hills. The wronged queen fled to her father, who attacked the eastern frontier of Herod's domains. It was part of the duty of the puppet kings of Palestine to keep this outer edge of empire at peace, and not wantonly to provoke border hostilities.

It was as part of his anxious attempt to meet the menace of the desert tribe that Herod was in occupation of his fortress of Machaerus, a stronghold built with others by his father to bind the most insecure frontier in the Middle East. It was not safe to leave the unpopular Herodias in the royal residence at Tiberias. That is why she was present in the officers' mess in the fortress keep.

John lay below for no other reason than that he had greeted the royal crime with his characteristic denunciation.

He described the deed in plain frank terms, its vicious licence for what it was. He pilloried the culprits before a land not insensitive to moral issues. Herod, too, had his memories. He was more easily touched than the hard woman who held him. Perhaps he wavered. Some deep apprehension over the security of her own vicious position may have driven Herodias to her implacable hatred. She had won much, and had no intention of weakening. Herodias is a spectacle of what a damned soul can become.

43 : Salome

Proverbs 28.1–18

We are still in the border banqueting hall within the Machaerus fort. The grim scene left its mark on history, and we turn the spotlight now on one of the figures on that evil stage, now on another. Salome is not actually named, but is known well enough, and named in Josephus. We have already looked at the drama's cruel end, but it is worth looking closer at the third actor in the scene. Nothing more basely vicious can well be imagined. Herodias knew the carnal lures by which she had trapped Herod. She had only one possible lower level to which it was possible to sink—to use her own daughter's voluptuous person to lead Herod to a deed of blood.

The girl may have been sixteen or seventeen years of age with all of her mother's sultry beauty. She glided in under the light of the lamps and the torches, demanding all eyes. The buzz of conversation, the drunken laughter, died. It was such an exhibition as that which Vashti scorned. Whirling, writhing, the slim girl danced some vicious dance, casting aside veils and robes to some bold, base climax of carnality.

Fired, half-maddened by the spectacle, which Herodias, with deep insight into what he was, had known so well how to arrange, Herod made his mad promise. Let her ask anything at all. Herodias had her moment and dictated the answer: 'The head of John the Baptizer'. The trap closed on a vicious coward. But there was still one way out. Physically the Herods were not cowards, but there is a distinction between physical and moral courage. Pride, as we have seen, dictated the final decision. At that point Herod virtually died. When he met Christ, He had no single word for him.

But our light was on Herodias' daughter, her mother's tool of evil, her mother's corrupted slave. She was as old, perhaps, as the Madonna. See how two lives can part. Vice in her limbs, words of blood on her young lips, Salome is a pitiable sight. The word for peace (shalom) is embedded in her name, but she brought no peace, carried none within her when she moved out of the story to be the wife of her grand-uncle Philip, the tetrarch. She has the odd distinction of giving Oscar Wilde a theme for a drama, banned from the British stage in less 'permissive' days. She remains a fearful example of what a bad woman can do to her own flesh and blood.

44 : Philip and Andrew

John 6.1–59

The feeding of the five thousand made a vivid impression on those who were present, and the story found its way, with variety of emphasis, into the writings of all the four evangelists. John's story is remarkable for both introduction and sequel. He it is who reveals how the imagery of the bread was taken up in the Capernaum synagogue in a notable discourse. He also describes a brief interchange of words which preceded the event.

Andrew and Philip play a part. There was a very considerable crowd in the lakeside meadow, and Jesus turned to Philip with a practical question. John remembered Philip vividly as an able and notable man. He came from Bethsaida, and was one of the first to be called (**1**.43 f.); he was instrumental in bringing Nathanael to Christ (**1**.45–49); he was chosen by the small group of Greeks to gain an interview (**12**.20–23); by a plain, direct question to Christ, he occasioned a remarkable saying (**14**.8 f.). And it is quite in character that Philip should be the object of the question which the Lord now asked.

He was right. As He had guessed, Philip had anticipated the problem, and had the basic cost worked out. It is possible to work out an approximate modern equivalent. A denarius, lamentably rendered 'penny' in the common English version, and not better translated by the shillings and dollars of other attempted equivalents, was a day's labouring wage, the sort of labouring wage which in a ruthless economy might have justified Karl Marx' 'iron law of wages'. Viewed even thus austerely, two hundred denarii was a sum beyond the resources of the apostles' band.

Philip gave his calculated reply, and Andrew facetiously pointed out that there was, in fact, a small supply available: 'There is a lad here who has five barley loaves and two fish . . .' He pauses when Jesus turns attentively, and takes him seriously, on which he lamely continues: 'But what are they among so many?'

Observe the fresh humanity of it all. There is no by-passing the miracle in the events which followed. It is told in plain factual language by the four witnesses. There is no difficulty provided Christ was indeed Christ, and all that which He claimed to be (John **1**.3). And if He was less than that, the whole fabric of Christian doctrine disintegrates. Before we leave these central chapters of the Gospel we shall look at the character of Christ, though to be sure, its presence haunts the whole story. But first a glance at a boy and a crowd.

45 : Child in the Crowd

Matthew 14.15–21; 26.26–30; Luke 9.10–17

A child played a part in the miracle of the loaves and the fishes. In a multitude of children's talks the small hero of the lakeside story has appeared as 'the little boy who gave his lunch to Jesus', but in fact five barley loaves and two fish would be a considerable picnic meal, even for a lad with a healthy appetite. It is more probable that the child was one of the many likely to haunt the outskirts of any Eastern crowd with small wares for sale. The unexpected influx of potential customers would stir more than one lonely cottage to baking and some attempt to turn the situation to profit.

So it came about, through this small link in the chain of circumstance, that the Lord obtained by gift or purchase the provision He needed. Matthew's account contains the vital phrase: 'Bring them here to me' (**14**.18). The small resource which was available passed into His creative hands. A divine principle of action seems apparent in the story. God seems to demand some point of entry into the world, some bridgehead of action. To bring blessing to mankind He seems to require some surrendered trifle, some shred of experience, some 'widow's mite', a small parcel of bread and fish, a sorrow, a pain, a joy. Given utterly to God the inconsiderable thing becomes active and fruitful in His hands. In Luke's account the key verse is **9**.16.

The blessing was no doubt the beautiful Jewish grace: 'Blessed art Thou, O Lord, our God, King of the Universe, who bringest forth bread from the earth.' On affluent societies the poignancy of such gratitude is lost. And note, in the midst of such prodigality, the Lord's care that nothing should be lost. The Jew, on a journey, always carried a 'cophinos', or rush-woven basket, in order to avoid buying Gentile food. The Twelve were thus equipped and supplied themselves for the morrow. Our wasteful society might note the fact. Waste is unchristian.

46 : The Crowd

Matthew 9.35–38; Mark 6.30–44

We have remarked upon the human simplicity of the four accounts of the lakeside picnic-meal. The whole experience must have remained a peculiarly vivid memory. Mark's account is specially vivid. Tradition has it, as we have seen, that Peter was Mark's informant, and one can catch the colourful language of the fisherman behind the evangelist's narrative. Verses 39 f., for example, run literally: 'He commanded them to make them all sit down in dinner-parties on the green grass. And they all sat down like beds of flowers in hundreds and fifties.' John also remembered that 'there was much grass in the place'. Here, surely, is the eye-witness who remembered what the spring-green hillside looked like when the fifty or more picnic-parties splashed the turf with the bright hues of their garments. In fact, the phrase runs literally 'they sat down in flower-beds'. That was the thought that struck the watching Peter. The fare was simple enough, a relish of dried or salted fish and barley bread. Barley, as we saw in the tale of Gideon's Midianite, was the cheaper grain, despised by the eaters of the wheaten flour. Christ by-passed luxury, and limited His miracles to the provision of bare need. Economically, He ordered His own men to fill their kits for the morrow's sustenance. Waste has no part in His programme, nor would He have His own look upon God as the indulgent Provider of that which men's own efforts, toil, and enterprise can produce. Providence does not assist the idle. The crowd in the Gospels is sometimes pathetic, 'like sheep without a shepherd' (Matt. **9**.36; Mark **6**.34), sometimes a disturbing presence shouting royal slogans which they did not understand, sometimes a deadly and a sinister force calling for Barabbas, and death for Christ . . . Crowds move like a spectre through history, manipulated by dictators, slaughtered to promote the evil of kings—and pitied by Christ. Crowds are disloyal and self-seeking, as ready to shout 'Crucify' as to call 'Hosanna'. Crowds disappoint (John **6**.26), take their morality from the lowest elements among them (Mark **15**.29 f.), follow designing men (Acts **19**.23–41), and are altogether unlovely. It behoves us to discipline disgust and pray the prayer of Christ (Matt. **9**.38).

47 : Greater than All

Matthew 10.32–42; 11.20–30; 12.1–8

We are not attempting, as we assemble the characters of the Bible, to unravel all the chronological problems involved. To integrate all the events of John's Gospel is a task of very great difficulty, for John wrote with other ends in view than an ordered sequence of events. Nevertheless, picking our way through the four Gospels, we are taking general account of the movement of time, and over the next thirty or forty studies shall move up to the triumphant entry to Jerusalem, and then move with all four evangelists through the events of the Passion Week.

The character of the Lord Himself has not engaged our special attention, but at this point we may pause to consider the significance of some astounding statements He was beginning to make, for the words throw light not only on His person but on the character of those who heard His words and reacted to them. Christ was far from unexpected at His coming. Apart from the learned in the law the common folk awaited Him. Says the Samaritan woman at the well, 'I know that Messiah is coming.' A fisherman says to his brother:

'We have found the Messiah.' The gossiping crowd in the Jerusalem streets say, 'When Christ comes, will He do more miracles than these?' Yet His coming and His character ran contrary to all the ideals and hopes of all but those who had eyes of the soul to see with. They looked for a Messiah who would bow the knee in humility before God, but who would walk like a king before men. But He held His head high before God. 'I and my Father are one,' He calmly asserts, and, 'He who has seen me has seen the Father.' He dares to look up into the face of Perfect Holiness and say, 'I glorified thee on earth.' Yet before men He chose service. As though indifferent to the longing for freedom that burned in the nation's heart He bade them render to Caesar the things that are Caesar's, and instead of turning His power against the Roman He used it on the sick. 'I am meek,' He avers, 'and lowly of heart.' It was obvious truth. Yet they speak of the mighty Law-giver, and He says, 'If you believed Moses, you would believe me', of the Prophet to the Gentiles, and He says, 'A greater than Jonah is here', of the Great King, and He claims a greatness more real than Solomon's.

48 : The Way and the Truth

Matthew 12.38–42; John 12.44–50; 14.1–6

The character of Christ is, in fact, the great miracle of the Gospels. No Jew could possibly have invented a person who ran so strongly counter to all that they had imagined of their Messiah. John, His forerunner, had not expected a Christ like this. The writers of the Gospels wrote of what they saw, but which they could not have anticipated. They wrote in spite of themselves. He contradicted their ideas in every point. Their father Abraham had spurned the bad king's gifts at the gate of Sodom: 'I could not take a thread or a sandal-thong.' Yet the Son of Man eats with publicans and sinners. Vengeance was a vice of which they made a virtue. In Study No. 31 we quoted Simonides' conversation with Ben Hur on revenge. How true it was! No ancient Jew would have invented a Messiah who bade one love his enemy and do good to those who used him despitefully. The typical Qumran community, as we saw, taught the precise opposite. They would look with contempt upon the humility before man of this strange Being who, it would have seemed to them, knew no humility before God. Even Paul, smitten in the High Priest's court, turned in a flame of indignation: 'God shall smite you, you whitewashed wall!' (Acts **23**.3). Yet this man, smitten and spat upon and crowned with thorns, utters not a word. It is impossible that the Christ of these pages could have been either the child of His age, or the literary invention of His contemporaries.

We have mentioned His startling claims. No mere man could make them and triumphantly sustain them in His day or ours. Greater than Solomon and Jonah, Moses' prophetic theme, pre-existing Abraham, all this is claimed with calmest confidence. He asserts that He is the penitent's way to God, the end of philosophy's quest, the goal of a world's desire, 'the way, and the truth, and the life' . . . the man from Galilee, whose father and brothers they knew! As if all light, all wisdom lived in Him, He opens His arms to groaning mankind and, 'Come to me,' He cries, 'all who labour and are heavy laden, and I will give you rest', and yet of those who came He demanded an abandonment which only God has the right to claim, an allegiance which overrides all earthly affection. With no sense of incongruity, but with all the anguish of rejected love He weeps over Jerusalem, hard and priest-ridden. How often would He have gathered her penitents together, as mother bird her brood, but the city would not! Were this mere man who speaks, was there ever effrontery so preposterous?

49 : The Discoverers

Matthew 13.45, 46; John 6.60–69; Philippians 3.1–14

We have turned aside briefly in the last two studies to look more directly at the Lord Himself, and we have done so because so many of those who will move before us over the next group of studies are closely involved with Him, and show their human qualities and defects against the foil of His strange perfection.

A group of parables, those human stories so characteristic of His teaching, appear at about this point in Matthew's account, and from them we may lift one word-picture, that of a merchant who discovered a lovely treasure from the ocean, a pearl of rare beauty, lifted by some bold diver from the floor of the Red Sea or the Persian Gulf. Its worth so gripped the mind of one man, that he cast aside all his other possessions in his zeal to hold this surpassing prize.

So, said the Lord, is one who finds what God has to give. There was a time in the ministry of Christ when, in disillusionment over the nature of His Messiahship, some 'drew back and no longer went about with him'. Literally the text runs: 'They went to the things behind, and walked no longer with Him'—that is, associated publicly with Him no more. Sadly He turned to His men and said: 'You don't want to go away too, do you?' And Peter, with that sudden gush of love which so often marked him, said: 'Lord, to whom should we go? You tell us about a kind of life which is altogether different from this.' It was the pearl of great price.

Paul found it too, and tells in the third chapter of his letter to the Philippians how he sold all. Curiously enough the passage contains an echo of John in the language he uses. In John **6**.66 the phrase runs literally: 'They went to the things behind . . .' The defectors were not necessarily returning to blatant sin, not necessarily to the terrorism which Simon the Zealot had abandoned, or the tax-office which Matthew had left behind—simply to the ordinary, humdrum affairs of life which they had left for the wider vision. And Paul says of such matters, in his imagery of the chariot race, that the committed Christian, 'forgetting the things behind', presses forward to a surpassing prize (Phil. **3**.13). Merchant, Peter, Paul—let us stand with them, and hold in hand that which is worth all the life's devotion, 'to be found in Him', to be used of Him, to be part of the vaster purpose, to be numbered among God's Remnant.

Questions and themes for study and discussion on Studies 41–49

1. What damned Herod?
2. Do you think it is correct to say that a woman can sink lower and rise higher than a man?
3. Compare Herodias with Jezebel.
4. Philip's character: how can the Church use his type?
5. God's creative power in everyday life and our social usefulness.
6. The crowd in Scripture and in history.
7. The impact of Christ upon His contemporaries.

RIGHTEOUSNESS IN CHRIST

Sanctified in Christ

50 : A Holy Nation

Exodus 19

This chapter concerns the preparation of Israel for receiving the law of the covenant at Sinai. In accordance with the promise of Exod. 3.12 Moses brought the people to the mountain, which he ascended to meet with the Lord (1–3). There God reiterated His intention to take Israel for His own possession and to make them a holy nation of royal priests (4–6). As a holy nation their devotion to the Lord would distinguish them from the other nations, and they were to cultivate holiness in character, which would reflect God's own holiness. As a kingdom of priests they would enjoy the royal and priestly prerogative of access to God and were to bring other nations to the knowledge of God. Obedience to God's mandates and covenant fidelity were therefore essential. The theophany, or manifestation of God, promised by Him on the mountain (9) would create an indelible impression of the majesty of God and would confirm Moses as His spokesman.

The privilege and responsibility of being the people of God, however, demands a knowledge of God's character. It was especially important for Israel to appreciate His infinite holiness. This was impressed on the people by the summons to a three-day period of consecration expressed through the ritual washing of clothing and abstinence from sexual relations (10, 15). These actions did not confer on the people that inner holiness without which a man cannot see God, but they symbolized their position as a people 'sanctified' or set apart for the Lord. In addition, a fence was constructed around the base of the mountain to keep the people from approaching too near, since the descent of God would make the mountain the seat of His immediate presence, a virtual 'holy of holies' (12 f.). These regulations underscored God's unapproachable holiness and the necessity for the people to become a holy nation through their covenantal relationship to Him.

The storm phenomena, the thick cloud, the trumpet blast heralding a royal proclamation, Mt. Sinai wrapped in a mantle of smoke and fire while the mountain rumbled and quaked—all these convey a vivid impression of the awesomeness of the approach of God (16–20). The people were terrified, for their prior experience of deliverance from Egypt and guidance through the wilderness had failed to disclose the full character of God and what this demanded of them. Lest they should presume to violate God's commandment to maintain their distance because they enjoyed only outward cleansing, Moses was instructed to repeat the stricture against approaching the mountain (21–25). Between priest and people there was no essential difference: they were unprepared for standing in the presence of a holy God.

51 : Consecration to Service

Exodus 29

The consecration of Aaron and his sons to the priesthood further stresses that holiness of life which the service of God requires. By representative actions they are set apart for a ministry which demanded a right attitude of heart prior to approaching God (1–4). Investiture with the robes of his office served to recognize Aaron's authority to function for God (5 f.). 'The holy crown' was a golden tablet inscribed 'Holy to the Lord' (**28**.36 f.) which affirmed that he had been set apart for God. Anointing (7) pointed to the unction of God's Spirit upon him, equipping him to fulfil his responsibilities. Yet these actions did not make Aaron and his sons holy. The problem of sin and unbelief remained and was dealt with by a series of three offerings. By laying their hands firmly on the head of the sacrificial animals, they recognized that their sin had been removed by God (10–14), that their lives must now be dedicated to God (15–18), and that they had been consecrated to their charge (19–21). The placing of blood from the consecrating ram on the right ear, thumb and great toe (20) served to remind them that no man can hear God's word, or serve God, or walk with Him apart from His sanctifying action. The sprinkling of the person and garments with the remaining blood symbolized that God's claim extended to their whole person. They were by this action removed from among the people to a position where all they did was intended to proclaim to the people the way of holiness. Their hands could then be filled with the sacrificial offerings to be presented to God on behalf of the people (22–28). The repetition of these rites on each of seven days would convey to the priests and to the people that God had called them to be a holy and priestly nation (cf. **19**.5 f.).

The command to offer daily the morning and evening sacrifice together with cereal and drink offerings (38–42) was to teach the people that expiation, consecration to service, thanksgiving, and fellowship with God must be renewed continually. God's promise to meet with His people and to be their God (43–46), which brings the chapter to a close, is especially important because it reminds us that holiness is not simply a matter of ritual prescription but of God's indwelling presence.

Question: What is there in your life that declares to others that you have been set apart wholly for the Lord?

52 : Positioned in Christ

1 Corinthians 1.1–3, 26–31; 6.9–11

Israel's call to be a holy nation, like the prescriptions governing the service of God in the sanctuary, declared that men can draw near to God only if they are holy. By virtue of God's sovereign choice, Israel became the holy people in the sense that they were set apart for God. In the New Testament the people of God are described by the phrase 'those sanctified in Christ Jesus' (2). This description points to God's action in drawing men to Himself, and not any act or quality of their own, as the reason for the existence of the Church. Just as Israel was called to be a holy nation (Exod. **19**.6), Christians have been called to be holy persons ('saints'). Their lives are to be defined, not by their past, but by God's claim on them. That sanctification in this context describes the position enjoyed by believers rather than their moral condition was particularly evident at Corinth, where gross immorality could be found in the church (cf. **5**.1 f.; **6**.9 f., 15–20). Those who had become Christians in the port city could boast neither of their pedigree nor of the purity of their lives (26–29; **6**.9–11a). By birth, social status and behaviour they appeared to be disqualified from participation in the life of a people designated 'holy'. The sole explanation for their presence in the church was God's action in restoring men to Himself through Christ (30). Just as Christ became righteousness for the believer, so that God views him, not as he is in himself, but in Christ, so Christ becomes for him the holiness which he does not possess in himself. This means that while he is neither righteous nor holy in a moral sense, he enjoys the righteousness and holiness which permit him to approach God because he is identified with Christ (**6**.11). His relationship to Christ will, of course, be effecting his moral transformation as well. This transfer of the holiness of Christ to the believer who can lay no personal claim to holiness can take place only because Christ in His death satisfied the demands of God's holiness. For this reason pride and boasting are meaningful only when men lift up the Lord (31) through whom they enjoy life, righteousness, holiness and redemption.

Thought: The person who is claimed by God finds that all rival claims recede into insignificance.

53 : The Importance of the Incarnation

Hebrews 2.10–13; 10.1–18

In the course of a meditation on the Incarnation and death of Jesus (**2**.5–18), the author considers the appropriateness of God's plan (10). He finds appropriate the decision to have Jesus experience the suffering of death (9, 14) so that He would be perfectly qualified to be the Saviour of men. The result of this decision is contemplated under the category of sanctification (11–13). The one who sanctifies is Jesus who by His death consecrates men to the service and worship of God. By His action men are constituted a holy congregation (12). Those who are sanctified are the 'many sons' (10) whom God intends to bring into His glorious and holy presence. In response to Jesus' perfect obedience to the Father they are given to Him to form the family of God who exhibit their trust in the provision of God (13).

What the sanctification of the new people of God entailed is clarified by **10**.1–18. The inability of the repeated offerings of the old covenant permanently to remove the sin which separated the people from God is stressed (**10**.1–4, 11). The chief value of the daily sacrifices, the author suggests, was the continual reminder of the fact and guilt of sin (3). Since this awareness was renewed every time Israel returned to the altar, it was impossible for animal sacrifices to remove sin (4). What was required was that personal sacrifice which God willed for Christ, and for which He made preparation by appointing to Him the body of the Incarnation (5–9). Jesus' determination to do the Father's will (7, 9) accounts for the efficacy of the single sacrifice for sins which He offered (12–18). It made possible the actual assumption of the guilt of men by Him. Through the offering of His body in perfect conformity to the intention of God guilt was removed and men were consecrated to the service of God. Because He maintained His obedience to the point of death, no repetition of His sacrifice was necessary or possible. The sanctification of men secured by His submission is as complete as the sacrifice which effects it (14). This point is made in the contrast between the priest who *stands* daily at his service (11) and Christ who offered a single sacrifice for sin and then *sat down* because His service was completed. His enthronement at God's right hand declares His dignity and indicates that He is the mediator of the blessings of the new covenant promised in Jer. **31**.33 (16 f.). The promise which forms the climax of Jeremiah's prophecy, that after the new covenant is ratified God will not remember the sins of His now sanctified people (17), demonstrates that no further sacrifice for sin is required. Jesus is the Sanctifier and Perfecter of the people of God.

54 : A Royal Priesthood

1 Peter 2.4–10

A strong note of exaltation characterizes this charge to come to Christ with a full awareness of what God has been pleased to do through Him. The description of Jesus as 'that living stone' reflects the Christian understanding of Psa. **118**.22 (cited in v. 7) which speaks of the great foundation-stone of the Temple which the builders had failed to recognize. Isa. **28**.16 (cited in v. 6) shows that this text was early understood to refer to God who would establish His people if they would trust Him. Unbelief, however, is the occasion of ruin (Isa. **8**.14 f., cited in v. 8). Peter recognized that these passages had reference to Jesus Christ; He was rejected by men but chosen by God to build the new temple attended by a holy priesthood engaged in the offering of spiritual sacrifices which God will find acceptable. As Jesus is the 'living stone' (4), so Christians are 'living stones' (5), the building blocks of the new house where God will dwell with His redeemed people. The description of believers as 'a holy priesthood' engaged in sacrifice recalls the consecration of Aaron and his sons for service at the sanctuary (Exod. **29**). Peter has prepared for this designation by describing believers as those 'sanctified by the Spirit for obedience to Jesus Christ and for sprinkling with his blood' (**1**.2), even as Aaron had been set apart for priestly service by the anointing oil and the sprinkling of blood. Their sacrifices are 'spiritual' because they consist, not in meat, cereal or drink offerings, but in the praise and service of God prompted by the Spirit. The privileges and responsibilities of the old priesthood have been transferred through the mediation of Jesus to the new people of God.

This means that the promise of Exod. **19**.5 f. has been fulfilled. The remarkable fact is that the phrases which had dignified Israel as a royal priesthood and a people for God's own possession are now applied to Gentiles, as the citation of Hos. **2**.23 in v. 10 makes clear. High privilege can be forfeited. The cost of Israel's failure to recognize God's redemptive action in Christ was the loss of their status as the focus of God's loving concern for men. Now, former pagans, who had done what all men without God do (cf. **4**.3 f.), are entrusted with the mission of bringing the world to recognize the glory of God (9–12). They had become the objects of God's sanctifying work through the death of Christ. As Peter reflects on this his language is coloured by the institution of consecration through sacrifice (**1**.2, 18–20) and its intention, the recognition of the holiness of God which demands the creation of a holy people (**1**.14–16). This leads him to recognize the pertinence of Exod. **19**.6 to Gentile believers in Asia who formerly had no claim on God but now have been claimed by God and entrusted with the responsibility of being a royal priesthood.

Question: *If the Church has become the heir to the promises made to Israel, what is its responsibility to the Jewish community*?

Questions and themes for study and discussion on Studies 50–54

1. How may we come to a deeper appreciation of God's holiness apart from the experience of a theophany like that at Sinai?
2. Are there times of special encounter with God when we should prepare ourselves by a three-day period of consecration? If so, how should such a period of time be used?
3. What is the importance of symbolic actions in the Christian's life? For instance, what is symbolized in the ordination of a man to the ministry?
4. What can a Christian do to lessen the distance between the holiness he enjoys in Christ positionally and the lack of experiential holiness he finds in his life?
5. What bearing does the teaching of Hebrews on sanctification through Christ have on the problem of sin and guilt in modern society? How will you explain sanctification to a person who has little knowledge of Christ or the Bible?
6. What priestly functions have been entrusted to Christians today? Does the discipline of intercessory prayer express a priestly task?

CHARACTER STUDIES

55 : Characters of John's Gospel

John 1.1–18; 20.30, 31; 21.20–25

It may be appropriate at this point to turn solely to John's Gospel and find our next dozen or so characters in its pages, carrying the story which we have more frequently followed in the synoptists, up to the last entry into Jerusalem and the Passion week.

John's stories are from life, and that fact has had abundant demonstration. For the last forty years some tattered fragments of the New Testament have lain in the John Rylands library in Manchester. They include two broken pieces of John's Gospel which lay unnoticed for fifteen years, from the date of their acquisition in 1920 until 1935, when C. H. Roberts recognized their unique importance. There were pieces of ch. **18**, vs. 31–33, and 37, 38, and the handwriting could be dated in the principate of Trajan or of his successor Hadrian. Observe the significance of this. Trajan died in A.D. 117, Hadrian in A.D. 138. Pick a point in the middle of Hadrian's principate, say A.D. 126, when his British garrison was building that astonishing symbol of empire, the wall across northern Britain. At that time John's Gospel was known, and being copied in Egypt. On those two tiny pieces of brown papyrus much fantasy was wrecked, and notably the attempt of some to thrust the fourth Gospel deep into the second century.

They were, of course, not the only piece of archaeological evidence which set John's Gospel back in its traditional place, inside the lifespan of the one who professed to write it, the last surviving apostle. His story is no 'pious' fiction. It has, indeed, been cogently argued by the historian, A. T. Olmstead, that the narrative passages in John represent the very oldest written tradition, a theory which, were this the place to do so, we might support by the story of John **8.** John wrote to refute the heresies which, in the late evening of his life, were disturbing the peace of the Church. He chose his materials to that end, but also with an eye to those facets of truth which had meant much in two generations of experience. One such truth was that of regeneration and how one already old can be 'born again'.

John had a way of tying what he taught to the incidents in the Lord's life which first put the truth into words. That is how the story of the woman of Samaria was rescued from oblivion, and how we come to know of the Pharisee who came by night, and whose question put the image of rebirth into Scripture, the blind man who exasperated the Sanhedrin, the tales of Cana, Bethesda and Bethany. And so we learn of the author himself—an old man who did his life's best work in his nineties. But he must wait until we read his last letters.

56 : Wedding Guests

John 2.1–12; Exodus 20.1–12

Cana lies on the hill slopes some four miles from Nazareth if the site is correctly identified. It is on the road to Tiberias. It is said to be Nathanael's village, a place of fertility and shady fig-trees (**1**.48, **21**.2).

It is not unlikely that the sudden and perhaps unexpected arrival of the Lord's party at the wedding was the occasion of the social disaster which befell the poor little household. Hence the anxious urgency with which Mary came to Him. In the lives of those who receive Him Christ causes no difficulty with which He is not richly able to deal.

But what of His reply to Mary? Was He harsh with His mother? The RSV, far from clearing up the AV (KJV) makes the words sound even more irritable. The Greek expression for 'What have I to do with thee?' is literally, 'What to you and to me?' Note it carefully. It means, 'What is there in common to you and to me?' Now, undoubtedly in John's story those words occur, but it is not at all improbable that John was literally translating a remark in Aramaic which ran, 'What is that to you and me?' and that He did not mean the words to be taken in the usual idiomatic sense. This version, which Nonnus accepted in the second century, and Luther at the time of the Reformation, at least clears up the story. Mary comes to Jesus. 'They have no wine,' she whispers. He replies, 'We are guests. What is that to you and me? My hour', He adds, 'is not yet come.'

That is, 'When I give a feast there will be no such accident.' When He did, in the upper room, there was plenty for all. However, as mothers do, giving no time for refusal, she says to the servants, 'Do whatever he tells you,' and hurries off. He smiles and complies. The word 'woman' had no harshness. In the tenderest scene in the *Iliad,* where Hector bids goodbye to Andromache on the walls of Troy, the hero addresses his wife as 'Woman'.

It is a vivid human little story, the Son, a trifle whimsical, the mother, bustling and certain of His unfailing help, the best man with his lame joke, perennial feature of wedding feasts . . . Phillips' 'ring of truth' is in every phrase.

57 : Nicodemus

John 3.1–16; Ezekiel 36.25–27; 37.1–10

Nicodemus came to Christ in desperate earnestness. He was a Pharisee, and for all the name of obloquy which the sect acquired through their participation in a mighty crime, the Pharisee had vowed to perform all the Law. He was a man to whom religion was everything. He came against all habit. 'Are you *the* teacher of Israel?' Christ asked him. He used the definite article, let it be noticed. Usually people came to Nicodemus. And he came by night, not in search of concealment, but of privacy. He came with a question.

The question was probably the one which tore at the Jew's mind: 'When, when, will God act, and restore the kingdom to Israel?' The Lord sensed its presence in the mind of Nicodemus, He saw it shaping on the lips of the grave man before Him, and interrupting him after his polite preamble He said: 'In solemn truth I tell you, unless a man be born again he cannot see the kingdom of God.' The emphasis lay on the last words. It is the lordship of God which matters, but the popular view of Israel's role meant little more than the pre-eminence of Israel.

The visitor was annoyed to be thus cut short, and pretended not to understand. But of course he understood the figure. He knew the Old Testament by heart. Any tag of quotations from some well-known, familiar passage sets the mind of a scholar racing along the lines of the text. A clear reference to a context of habitual meditation raises the whole associated complex of ideas to the mind. Nicodemus knew that Christ was taking him in thought to passages in Ezekiel, in what we call chapters **36** and **37** of that prophet's book. In the quiet night it was in the context of those well-remembered passages that Nicodemus received the answer to the question he was not permitted to ask, and much more truth beside . . . They spoke of life renewed but life renewed by the breath of God's Spirit in response to prayer.

The play of mind with mind continues and we need not follow further. 'How comes this to pass?' said Nicodemus, now alert to follow the imagery evoked. He is taken to the tale in the Book of Numbers in which those who looked up in faith lived. So are men reborn and enter into eternal life, when their upreaching faith lays hold of the proffered grace.

Nicodemus went his way, and we shall meet him again. Was he convinced? It is a fair guess that he was (cf. **19**.39).

58: The Reborn

John 5.24; Romans 6.3–23

Read the famous sixteen verses again (John **3**.1–16). Nicodemus had his answer, and as he went away under the concealment of the night he may have heard on those uplands of the city the sigh of the night wind that had reminded him of Ezekiel. He had his answer. 'When will the kingdom be restored to Israel?' 'When God reigns in the lives of individual Israelites, and they glimpse the reality of the royal presence of God in their own deepest experience. That is when God will move again with restoration, Nicodemus, when the dry bones live once more in each surrendered life'. And as he walked home he may have grasped a truth, that God gives more abundantly than our asking, and always answers a question more comprehensively than the questioner could even imagine. There was to be a new race, regenerated characters, men who have 'looked' and 'lived'.

Rebirth establishes a new ancestry, a fresh pattern of genetics for the soul. We become that which lies at the core of the being, in 'the heart', if you will. If a principle of falsehood lies there it cannot do other than colour thought and emotion. It then flows into speech and action, and speech and action constitute what others see us to be, and call our character. Character, long enough maintained, becomes personality. The host of falsehood becomes a living lie, self-deceiving, unable to be true.

So, too, if hate is cherished in the centre of the being, or any other evil principle, it cannot be contained. It seeps abroad and eats up its host.

But so, too, with Christ. He is born again into whose life's inner depth Christ comes with power to renew. Once lodged there, He cannot be cabined or confined. He cannot be hidden. He breaks into thought, word, character, personality, until He overwhelms the whole—and yet, unlike the evil which can eat up a human being, obliterating, destructive, lethal, the indwelling Christ transforms by life's renewal. He is God's Creative Force, as the same John says in his Prologue. He makes the host who houses Him like Him, but paradoxically leaves the personality which He takes over more himself, more real, more alive than that person ever could have been when lost in the embrace of consuming death.

Such is the rebirth. Life's scattered remnants are re-articulated anew, each functioning in its appropriate place. The person is sinewed, fleshed, and equipped with sensitivity, energy, beauty. The integrated whole is made alive by the breath of God. Growth remains, as it awaits any new-born creature, but growth follows the assimilation of God's Living Bread, the Milk of His Word, the Meat of His Strength.

Questions and themes for study and discussion on Studies 55–58

1. Reality in John's narratives.
2. Christ's involvement in ordinary social life—what principles for ourselves can be gained from John **2**.1–12?
3. The relationship between knowledge and spiritual perception.
4. 'Rebirth' as a figure of speech.
5. 'Perish'—what does it mean?

RIGHTEOUSNESS IN CHRIST

Sonship and Inheritance in the Old Testament

59 : The Double Portion

Deuteronomy 21.15–17; 2 Kings 2.9–12

God graciously accommodates Himself to the level of our human understanding. He speaks in terms we can grasp from our experience of the family and of ownership of land. His intention is that we will finally perceive that He has been talking about our relationship to Him, but He patiently instructs us through the practical matter of relating to each other.

The domestic legislation of Deut. **21**.15–17 is designed to protect the right of the first son from a favouritism that would capriciously transfer his heritage to another. In the situation described the husband and father is not free to do what he desires. He must recognize the right of his first son to twice as much as his brothers receive since it will be his responsibility to care for the family after his father's death. By this restriction in personal freedom God shows that sonship is important to Him and that it implies both privilege and responsibility. He Himself remains the family head, and in the assignment of an inheritance His headship is to be recognized.

Elijah's relationship to Elisha was like that of a father to a son. It is possible that the gesture of casting his mantle over the younger man at the time of his call (1 Kings **19**.19) was a form of adoption, since Elisha left his family and ministered to Elijah from that time (1 Kings **19**.20 f.; 2 Kings **2**.1–6). Elijah recognized Elisha's right to the inheritance promised to the first son (9 f.). There is no evidence that he possessed land or wealth to bestow, but when he inquired what he should do for Elisha, his colleague promptly asked for the portion of the first son, a double share of Elijah's spirit. He was not asking to be twice as great as Elijah, but to be a worthy successor to the prophet's office and responsibility. The high privilege of sonship required nothing less. Elijah's response (10) indicates that it was not his prerogative to bestow such a heritage. Even as God had assigned to Elisha the position of son (1 Kings **19**.16) He alone could appoint him as heir. Sonship and inheritance find their ultimate source in God's sovereign decision.

Thought: Inheritance is never an end in itself, but only a means to service.

60 : A Question of Ownership

Numbers 34.1–15; Leviticus 25.23

People feel secure in the possession of land. It was not God's intention that Israel should find their security in their tribal portion but in their possession of Himself. For that reason He left nothing to the decision of men. He defined with precision the borders of the land of Canaan which would constitute the inheritance of the remaining tribes (**34**.1–12), since Reuben, Gad, and half of the tribe of Manasseh had received permission to settle in Transjordan (**32**; **34**.13–15). The determination of the portion to be inherited by each tribe through the casting of lots would remind Israel that it was God who defined the character of their inheritance and decided where they should settle. This procedure called for the recognition of His sovereign control over their lives and destinies, and served to exalt Him as God in Israel. It was imperative that the visible, tangible character of the land should not obscure the fact that God's people owe everything they enjoy to His gracious intervention in their lives.

This is made explicit in Lev. **25**.23: God is the owner of the land. Israel enjoys its inheritance not by virtue of prior ownership or conquest, but only because God chooses to bring them into His heritage. The terms 'strangers and sojourners' define them as persons without rights or claims. God permits them to be tenants on His land, providing they remain 'with' Him. The implication is that so long as they continue to recognize Him as Sovereign and maintain their covenant with Him faithfully they will enjoy possession of the land. But when the land displaces Him as the object of their affection it will be torn from them. The prohibition of the sale of the land further emphasizes that the land is the Lord's and that Israel does not have authority over it. They are called to recognize their dependence on God and the necessity of receiving from Him all that they need. It is therefore significant that the context of Lev. **25**.23 concerns the sabbatical year when the land is to be fallow and Israel must depend on the harvest of the sixth year to sustain them until the harvest of the eighth year is gathered (Lev. **25**.1–22). God calls for complete trust in His provision for our needs, whether that need is for righteousness, holiness, or physical sustenance.

Question: *To what degree has God's ownership over your life been made real?*

61 : The Praise of God

Deuteronomy 4.32–40; Psalm 105.1–11

Recital of God's mighty acts was an important element in the life of Israel. His intervention in the affairs of nations declared Him to be the Lord of history, who had chosen the Israelites to be the object of His particular favour. Moses appeals to the experience of the wilderness generation as proof of the majesty of God and of Israel's unique privilege (32–39). The experience of the people at Sinai (33, 36, cf. Exod. **19**.9, 19), like the deliverance of the enslaved nation from Egypt (34, 37) and the dispossession of the nations in Canaan (38), demonstrated that the Lord alone is God (35, 39). He had rescued Israel from the mightiest empire of that day for the sole reason that He loved the patriarchs and chose their descendants as His people (37). The discipline imposed through the law-statutes of the covenant (cf. v. 36) expressed God's electing love as thoroughly as did the events of the Exodus. The proper response to the acknowledgement of the Lord as God is obedience to His will (40). Covenant privilege entails covenant responsibility.

Reflection on the acts of God leads spontaneously to doxology (Psa. **105**, 1–11). The psalmist's call for a public proclamation of God's deed among all nations has a missionary intention (1). Witness, however, is the prelude to worship, which is contemplated under the aspect of singing (2), praise (3), prayer (4) and recital for purposes of remembrance (5 f.). The remembrance by the people of God's intervention in the days of the Exodus (5) is balanced by God's remembrance of the covenant made with Abraham (8–11, 42, cf. Gen. **15**.18), which found a point of focus in the promise of the land of Canaan as an inheritance. The pattern of repeated promise to Isaac, Jacob and the wilderness generation proves that God never forgot His covenant and designates His people as those who live in relationship to His promise. The subsequent rehearsal of Israel's history from the patriarchal period to the occupation of the land (12–45) is a recital of God's unwavering fidelity to His promise (42) and evokes a response of praise. The inheritance points beyond itself to the God who keeps His word and excites in His people unexcelled joy and praise.

Thought: *The antidote to anxiety and complaint is recital and doxology.*

62 : The Ultimate Inheritance

Numbers 18.8–20; Joshua 13.14, 32, 33

Although God decreed that Israel should inherit the land, it was crucial that they should recognize that He Himself was their ultimate inheritance. A visible reminder of this fact was given to them through the tribe of Levi which had been set apart for service in the tabernacle. In distinction from the other tribes, they were given no inheritance in the land (Num. **18**.20; Josh. **13**.14, 33). Aaron and his sons, unlike the priests of the surrounding nations, are not to become wealthy landholders. The Levites are to be supported by the tithes of the nation (Num. **18**.21, 24), while the priests are to be fed from the altar (Num. **18**.8 f.; Josh. **13**.14). Num. **18**.8–20 is largely concerned with the consecrated offerings by fire (8–11), the first fruits of oil, wine, grain and produce (12 f.), the gifts offered to God as response to a vow (14), and the flesh of first-born cattle, sheep and goats (15–18) which were to become their property. The description of these items as 'most holy' and the regulation that they are to be eaten in 'a most holy place' (9 f., 17, 19) stems from the fact they were first offered to God. All such sacrifices and gifts belong in an absolute sense to Him. They become the portion of the priests and their families only by divine appointment as God enters into an indissoluble covenant with Aaron and his descendants (19).

These measures reduced the priesthood to total dependence on the Lord, so that they might find in Him their inheritance

(20; Josh. **13**.33). By the solemn promise that 'I am your portion and your inheritance' (20) they are designated a people for whom He will care in a particular way. The priests are to possess *nothing* but what they receive from Him. But in their possession of Him they find that they have received *everything*. No object of personal possession which might detract them from their enjoyment of God stood in their way. Consequently, their presence among the tribes constituted a continual reminder that the land cannot be Israel's ultimate inheritance. The heart knows longings which can be satisfied only in the possession of God.

Thought: *Our unconditional surrender to God is the only appropriate response to His willingness to give Himself to us.*

63 : The Enjoyment of God

Psalm 16

What it means to enjoy God as your inheritance is clarified by this prayer as David reflects on his own experience of the Lord. The cry for preservation in the context of the threat of death (1, 9 f.), together with the figure of God as a tower of refuge (1) or military champion (8), suggests that this psalm was composed when David was a fugitive and was reduced to life as an outlaw. The fragile character of human life and the sense of imminent danger with which he lived sharpened his awareness of his need for God's protection. David knew that the Lord was his sole resource, and he found Him all-sufficient. Forced to flee from the court of Saul, he now recognized as the true nobility in Israel those who feared God (3). He could delight in them because he shared with them a common faith. Rejecting the false gods of Philistia (4), David found the satisfaction of his heart in the possession of the Lord (5 f.). To express his feelings he uses the figure of a banquet and an inheritance. 'My cup' in v. 5 shows that the parallel expression 'my chosen portion' has reference to a portion of food. David had found that all he needed to satisfy hunger and thirst fully was the enjoyment of God. It was like being entertained at a banquet. 'My lot' and 'the lines' in vs. 5 f. refer to the fact that an inheritance was measured out line by line (cf. Amos **7**.17).

His heritage was the Lord, and harshness of life in the wilderness could not dull his sensitivity to the joy and pleasure he experienced in the presence of God (6, 11).

David's statement in v. 5 should be compared with Num. **18**.20 where God says to Aaron and his sons, 'I am your portion and your inheritance.' They were *commanded* to find their sufficiency in Him. Here David *confesses* that he has chosen to find in God his portion and inheritance, not because of a command, but because he has come to know God as *his* Lord (2). His experience of God's counsel and correction (7) assured him of God's presence. Moreover, he had learned that his security depended on the Lord (8–11). Hidden behind God his Champion, who stands at all times between him and his foes, David knew the enjoyment of gladness (9) even when his life was severely threatened. God would preserve him from death (10) and lead him into His presence where the man of faith experiences a satisfaction that defies description. The terms 'fullness of joy' and 'pleasures for evermore' (11) only hint at an ultimate fulfilment. In v. 8 David finds God at *his* right hand to protect him in conflict. In v. 11 the conflict has been forgotten as he finds himself at *God's* right hand open to the enjoyment of God. The early apostles found David's statement perfectly fulfilled in the resurrection of Jesus (Acts **2**.25–28; **13**.35, cf. 1 Peter **1**.3 f.), which provides a sufficient reason for our security and joy as Christians when our life is threatened by death.

Thought: *How often it requires a reduction to dire circumstances before we will fully appreciate how wonderful it is to know the Lord!*

Questions and themes for study and discussion on Studies 59–63

1. Should the principle of a double portion of an inheritance to the oldest son because of his responsibility to care for the family be enacted as law in our society? What implications would this have for the problem of the care of the aged?
2. What implications for Christian stewardship can be drawn from the principle that God is owner of Israel's inheritance?
3. What can be done to encourage the praise of God in personal and corporate worship? What forms can praise assume?

CHARACTER STUDIES

64 : The Woman at the Well

John 4.1–30

The well is still to be seen outside the little town, walled, padlocked and sequestered after man's common fashion. It was the heat of the day, because the woman who came down for water had no wish to face the looks of the other women of the town, nor to hear their covert sneers. Immoral, obscure, ignorant, flippant, she stood in complete contrast with the gentlemanly scholar Nicodemus. Yet both stories follow on from John's remark in **2**.25. Observe how differently the Supreme Teacher deals with the two persons. In Nicodemus He spoke in the imagery of Scripture. He could not do so with the outcast alien. Meeting her at the level of her understanding and her need, the Lord asked for a drink. Proceeding no doubt to give the stranger the drink He craved, the woman is unable to resist a little sarcasm. 'You, a Jew, asking for a drink from me, a Samaritan woman!' The Lord showed no shadow of annoyance, but answered with a disarming word. 'If you knew . . .' He said, and curiosity as old as Eve was stirred. Eve's curiosity led to death; the Samaritan's to life.

Like the prodigal, the woman may have glimpsed a way out of physical distress. Her reply in v. 15 may, on the other hand, have been no more than a down-to-earth comment on Christ's strangely mystical language. The time has come to shock her into earnestness, so the Lord lays His finger on the deeper pain and shame of her disordered life (16). He does that sometimes, especially when in folly we refuse to face the reality of our sin and pathetic rebellion. So Nathan confronted David. A proper relationship is now established, but she still tries to evade the *personal* issue by provoking a *theological* debate on an issue of division and controversy between Jew and Samaritan. The reply out-distances her understanding, so the woman seeks to close the conversation on the comfortable ground that there is much mystery, but some day all will be made clear—'when Messiah comes'.

Hence the sudden revelation. Humbled at last, convinced, and awake to something real, saving, new, the woman, forgetting the task of drudgery at home, hurries away to tell the town. At the well the mystified disciples wait. It is down the hill, and out of sight of the village. Over the brow of the rise the woman has disappeared.

65 : The Samaritans

2 Kings 17.24–34; John 4.31–42; 8.48

Samaria had suffered, seven centuries before, as the northern kingdom of the divided land. Devastated, depopulated, and then resettled with mixed or alien breeds, the province had met the scorn and contempt of Judah, whose divine calling was surely rather to love, and to share the knowledge of their God.

The Jews, whose national integrity had endured a century longer until they, too, went into exile, had lost their vast opportunity. Hence the division and the scorn of the Lord's day, and the pathetic situation which He sought to bridge. The woman at the well was to be His bridgehead of conquest.

He found a ready audience. Samaria, under-privileged and not possessing the full canon of the Old Testament Scriptures, was hungry for the truth of God with an eagerness not felt in hard, contentious Jerusalem. Hence the compulsion which took the Lord that way. His path ever lies near the place of man's need and aspiration. The ready response to the woman's timid testimony shows how ripe was the harvest. The Lord's conversation shows how conscious He was of the fact. The theme of 2.25 still binds the story together. By the well He prolonged the discussion with the puzzled disciples until the Samaritans came into sight round the corner of the hill. He then bade them lift their eyes and see the harvest waiting among the alien and the despised. Lands of ancient privilege, which have long known the gospel, and treated its old invitations with scant respect, should note the story. Let it also be noted that evangelism is a task for toil and dedication, a sequence of planting and reaping for which hands are all too few. Under its urgency the Lord ignored His weariness and His need for food and rest. The Church too often lacks what Jowett called 'a passion for souls', that deep and earnest desire by all means to win others to Christ by their own loyalty and love.

We hear no more of the people of the little town. We do not know whether the woman of the wellside conversation was received as a sister among them, her integrity restored, her life remade. We do not know what happened to the man who shared her corruption. We only know that, unlike the Gadarenes who preferred their swine, the Samaritans wanted Christ to stay with them.

66 : Herod's Officer

John 4.43–54; Isaiah 55

The scene of action changes to Galilee and the succession of incidents which forms the theme of chs. **3** and **4** ends with the story of a desperate man. He was an officer of Herod's court, and far removed in social status from both Nicodemus and the unnamed Samaritan outcast. Overwhelmed by personal sorrow, he sought Christ's aid with urgency. Testing not infrequently goes with blessing, and the man from Capernaum was tried, first with apparent refusal, and then with a Divine response which went all against his expectations. Like Naaman, he was told to trust forthwith, and act upon that faith. The pattern is common enough in God's dealings with men. God's delays are God's disciplines, and He seldom answers prayers according to our small, and at times presumptuous, specifications. 'His plans are not like our plans', as Moffatt renders Isa. **55**.8. They are, in fact, infinitely superior, and delightful to the soul who finds his place in them. His answers, like His tarrying, are designed to stimulate a trusting faith. Capernaum was 25 miles away, and the man went home without haste. He remembered that day, not only for a blessed boon granted, but as his life's greatest spiritual experience. Life is enriched if it is lived in the wonder of such faith. There is joy in the life which has learned to look for God's solutions, God's transformation of our pain, God's unforeseen blessings.

Revert again to the thought that the statement in **2**.25 is a thread which links a series of characters and events together. He 'knew what was in man', and so could deal on varied planes with the superbly trained scholar, the rejected woman, and the incisive executive who hurried up from Capernaum to Cana to beseech His help. In each case His word and His challenge were adapted to personality and training. In the rabbi He called upon that awareness of spiritual truth, and the medium which contained it, which was the very pattern of all His thought. He took the Samaritan woman, and cut away all her pathetic posing and pretence until she became conscious of the simple fact of her sin. The royal officer of Capernaum was a clear-thinking, strong, plain man. He had come to Cana with one sharply conceived purpose. Like Luke's centurion he was a man who understood authority. The Lord called him to a firm, strong step of faith. He frequently acts like this, addressing the best in us, calling for the highest response—but never beyond that to which the spirit can rise.

67 : The Man by the Pool

John 5.1–18

Many strange things have been said of the fourth Gospel. Hostile criticism has sought in vain, as we have remarked, to thrust its composition into the second century and outside the possible life-span of its aged author. If it could but be proved that the Church of the first decades of the second century, among whom were those whose parents and grandparents remembered the apostles, had accepted as genuine the blatant falsehoods of one who pretended to be the revered and well-remembered John, and who untruthfully professed to have stood bravely by the Cross, and to have run with Peter to the Empty Tomb, what opportunity then takes shape for 'new theologies'! Anyone, in this or any other century, would be free to rewrite the story of Christ, and put upon His lips whatever sheer romance, narrow prejudice, or special pleading, he might at any time imagine that the Lord might have said in any other age than in His own.

Archaeology has frequently played a role in combating such fancies, and the story of the Bethesda well is one such case. It was Loisy, the French liberal scholar, who suggested that John, or whoever wrote under that name, had altered the traditional tale to include the five colonnades. This, of course, was to represent the five books of the Law which

Jesus had come to fulfil. Of this the sick man was himself a symbol. Recent excavations have revealed that, before A.D. 70, there existed a rectangular pool with a colonnade on each of the four sides, and a fifth across the middle.

The competitive miracle of v. 4 remains a difficulty. It is not consistent with the spirit of the Bible. The presence of such an anomaly in the text of Scripture would puzzle and confuse were it not for one fact. Some of the most ancient and important manuscripts do not include v. 4, hence its omission in the RSV. It is this verse which is the stumbling block. The fact that the pool was considered a place of healing is of no significance, although it is noteworthy that the Lord uttered no word of confirmation. Mind is strangely potent over matter, and healing may well have taken place there. It may even be true that at times gaseous exhalations from the pool made the waters more potent, or stimulated faith more effectively. It is the angel with his periodic visit, the apparent scramble for a gift of God, which constitutes the difficulty. Strong textual objection to v. 4, supported by the exegetical difficulty, make a very strong case for the exclusion of the verse. It is of the exact nature of a 'gloss.' A copyist writes a traditional explanation in the margin of his manuscript, and someone else, copying from him, includes the explanation mistakenly in the text. It is to be noted that the Lord did not use the pool to heal the paralytic, but gave the grace of His divine help as grace is always given—that is, in response to an act of faith.

68 : The Man in the Temple

John 5.19–29

Looking at the background of the story and the difficulty of the text we have lost sight of the despairing man who had hoped so pathetically for healing at the pool. The Lord does not argue against the common belief in a strangely competitive miracle, just as in a later healing He descends to the level of the blind man's feeble faith (9.6–12). He healed in spite of it. In effect the Lord asks: 'Do you *want* to get well?' The man's answer shows that he was eager enough for healing, but lacked strength or the help of another. The Lord's command to him to arise gave him both, and more.

Straightaway he was made whole. This man, now 'found in the Temple', no doubt in grateful prayer, is bidden: 'Sin no more.' Medical science is increasingly impressed by the fact that sickness of the mind and spirit promotes the breakdown of the body, and the command seems to indicate that the sick man's paralysis was the final physical fruit of a tormented and sin-sick soul. His sin was a matter between himself and God. No public mention is made of it (6, 8, 14), but permanent cure depended upon spiritual victory. God's blessings are for those who trust and obey.

All good turns to evil in the hands of evil men. The beginnings of conflict arose from the Lord's loving kindness. The path to Calvary began in the Temple court, and by the Bethesda pool. John's method is often to attach great discourses to the incidents out of which they arose. The Jews, who were trained in symbolic language, would see the point of the Lord's words to the case of the paralysed man. The concentrated statement before us contains, firstly, a new version of the Sabbath. The institution of a day of rest was not intended to paralyse godly and beneficent action, but to energize it. Secondly, observe a clear claim to Divine worship. The Lord claimed to reproduce visibly among men the work of the Father, to bestow life, to execute judgement, and to raise the dead. And are we not still outworking the truth enunciated in **2**.25? The Lord 'knew what was in the man'.

Questions and themes for study and discussion on Studies 64–68

1. Water as a symbol in Scripture.
2. The Jews and the Samaritans. Duty and failure.
3. 'Testing not infrequently goes with blessing.'
4. How did the Lord deal with the Bethesda pool? What of Lourdes and similar phenomena?

RIGHTEOUSNESS IN CHRIST

Sonship and Inheritance in the New Testament

69 : A Question of Parentage

John 8.31–58

A son is a reflection of his father. The dispositions he displays and the direction of his life disclose what he has learned from his father. These two statements sum up the sharp exchange between Jesus and certain Jews who had believed in Him (31) but who found His teaching on freedom and bondage offensive and whose 'belief' was therefore exposed as superficial. They claimed to be sons of Abraham (33, 39) and repudiated any suggestion that they needed to experience freedom (33). Regarding sonship as a question of descent, they failed to recognize that beyond the accidents of historical existence there is a lineage which can be traced to God or to Satan. While Jesus acknowledged their physical ties with Abraham He exposed the deeper issues of character, intention and performance.

The freedom of which He spoke was freedom from sin which identifies the son in distinction from one who is a slave (32, 34–36). Only if He who is the Son of God in a unique sense liberates men can they enjoy the status of sons of God (36). The rapidity with which the Jews became incensed and murderous (37, 40, 59) indicated that they were not authentic sons of Abraham—to judge by character and performance. While Jesus follows His Father's example, they follow the example of their father (38). Their parentage can be traced to the devil, who was associated with murder and lying since he brought death to Adam and his descendants with his subtle twisting of the truth (44 f., cf. Gen. **3**.4). The protest that 'we have one Father, even God' (41) is valid only if those who claim to be sons of God recognize that Jesus is the unique Son whom the Father sent into the world (42). In point of fact they fail to recognize Jesus' words as the truth of God (43, 47) and they accuse Him of being a heretic who is possessed by a demonic spirit (48, 52). The ease with which they dismiss Jesus as deranged and dishonour Him demonstrates that Abrahamic descent is no guarantee of knowing the Father. It is the claim to know Him by men who dishonour His Son which proves them to be liars like their father (44, 55) and exposes them to the judgement by which the Father will vindicate His Son (50). Jesus' concern to glorify God, not Himself, validates His sonship and His mission.

The reference to Abraham in v. 56 looks back to the promise of blessing to the nations through the patriarch (Gen. **12**.2 f.) which will find its fulfilment in the death and resurrection of the Son. The argument runs: Abraham rejoiced to see My advent, and if you were really his sons you would share his joy. The response of these Jewish challengers of Jesus' sonship (57) indicates they do not understand His point. But when Jesus identified Himself by the divine name, 'I am' (58, cf. Exod. **3**.14), they saw immediately that He claimed for Himself the timeless quality of deity. Their determination to stone Him in accordance with the laws governing blasphemy (59) constitutes their final rejection of a sonship which could be conferred only through Him. They determine to be the slaves of sin rather than free sons in the household of God.

Thought: Slavery and freedom are matters of the heart, not of social or political standing.

70 : Sons of Abraham

Galatians 3.1–14

In Galatia Judaizers attempted to make Christian experience dependent on the forms and rites of Judaism. An insistence on circumcision (cf. **5**.2–6, 12) shows that they held that Gentiles must become full proselytes before they were qualified to be Christians. Paul refused to allow salvation to depend on anything more than faith in the finished work of Christ. In this letter he stresses the significance of Christ's death on the cross (**1**.4; **2**.20 f.; **3**.1, 13; **6**.12, 14, 17). The central importance of the cross is due to the fact that one is removed from the sphere of law only by death. Because the Son of God fully satisfied in His death the claims of the law, the law has no claim on Christians who identify themselves with Jesus in His death (**2**.19–21). The apostle's intention in **3**.1–14 is to remind the Galatians that this truth was validated in their own experience of faith.

When Paul proclaimed the meaning of Christ's death in Galatia, Gentiles had believed the truth (1). They were confirmed in their faith by reception of the Holy Spirit and by miracles (2, 5, 14). An acceptance of circumcision as the token of their submission to the law would affirm that Jesus' death on their behalf (**1**.4; **3**.1) had been insufficient by itself to guarantee their status as sons of God. Their own experience confirmed that it was in response to faith alone that they had been accepted by God (3).

Since the Judaizers made much of the Abrahamic covenant in their preaching of circumcision, Paul goes back to Gen. **15**.6 (6) to prove that 'it is men of faith who are the sons of Abraham' (7). Sonship is here defined in terms of having the same faith as that which characterized the father. Abraham's faith in the promise that Gentiles would receive blessing through him (8, cf. Gen. **12**.3) indicates that the heart of the gospel, justification on the ground of faith alone, was already known to him. Men of faith thus constitute a family of sons who may trace their lineage to Abraham, the man of faith *par excellence* (9).

The consequences of seeking justification on any other basis than faith are explored in vs. 10–14. While Gentiles who come to God as Abraham came, in the way of faith, may expect blessing (8), those who seek shelter in the law may anticipate only a curse, for Deut. **27**.26 brings a blanket condemnation on everyone who does not fulfil the whole law (10). Law requires a level of performance that no one can satisfy (11 f.). Jesus' death upon the cross indicates that He took the curse to Himself in order to exhaust its sting (13, citing Deut. **21**.23). Sonship can never depend on the level of our performance. It can rest only in Jesus' perfect satisfaction of the demands of God. Abraham's true sons will be those who place their faith in Jesus.

71 : The Inviolable Character of Promise

Galatians 3.15–29

Paul illustrates what he has been saying concerning sonship in the family of faith (6–14) by reference to the principle of inviolability once a man's will has been ratified (15). If tampering with the provisions of a will is criminal, we can be certain that the promise of God expressed in the solemn context of a covenant ceremony remains constant. The consideration of the Abrahamic covenant under the aspect of promise is not arbitrary, for Gen. **15**, which records the ratification of the covenant (Gen. **15**.17 f.), stresses God's promises to His servant (Gen. **15**.4 f., 18–21). These promises concern descendants and an inheritance, but they find their focus in Christ through whom the promises are finally realized (16). No subsequent action of God, like the giving of the Law at Sinai, could nullify the promises guaranteed by God's action (17). This implies that even as Abraham received his inheritance in the form of promise (18), so those who are his sons must expect to receive their heritage on the ground of promise alone.

The relationship between the Law and covenant promise is explored in vs. 19–29. There is no conflict between them (21) since each has its distinct function. The function of the Law was to expose transgressions, so that men would cling to the promise of God and not to a piety founded on merit (19). The Law was intended neither to impart life nor to compel obedience. This must be the work of God in response to the promise made to Abraham (21 f.). The Law, therefore, should be regarded as the gracious provision of God to restrain men from the consequences of their fallen condition until Christ came and displayed the character and extent of the promise (23 f.). The function of the promise was to thrust men upon God in a trust relationship. It pointed forward to the coming of Christ and affirmed that faith in the promise was the mark of the people of God. Paul uses the figure of the 'custodian' to represent the Law (24). The custodian was a slave assigned to escort an unwilling pupil to school, and in Greek drama a mask with a harsh demeanour was used for this character. In Paul's figure Christ (or faith, v. 25) is the schoolmaster who teaches us that we become sons through faith in God's fidelity to His promise. Incidentally, the use of 'schoolmaster' for the custodian in the AV (KJV) is somewhat misleading. The coming of faith (23) and the coming of Christ (24) are concurrent experiences for Christians. Submission to the schoolmaster is the mark of sons and releases them from the harsh treatment of the custodian (25 f.). Conversely, failure to appreciate the character of faith in Christ permits one to fall back into a neo-legalism which will restrict the exercise of responsible freedom. Paul insists that what he has been saying has reference to all classes of society (27 f.). Identification with Christ, to whom the promises made to Abraham were ultimately directed (16), is crucial because those who are Abraham's sons and daughters through faith become heirs precisely because of the inviolable character of the promise of God.

Thought: Those who find their support in the structures of legalism have never known the exhilaration of the life of faith.

72 : The Son as Heir

Galatians 4.1–10

Paul alluded to the pre-Christian experience of his readers under the figure of a harsh custodian compelling an unwilling pupil to attend the school of faith (**3**.23 ff.). The subsequent identification of the pupil as a son (26) and heir (29) was left unexplained. Paul therefore clarifies his figure in **4**.1 f. and then applies it to the Galatians (**4**.2–11). Designation as an heir permits access to the inheritance only if one is of legal age. If he is a minor the inheritance remains in the control of trustees and there is little difference in status between a slave and an heir (1 f.). Both must submit to discipline. Our experience as Christians is analogous to this, with one important qualification: we began as slaves (3). We were enslaved to certain 'first principles' of law or rudiments of conduct. (This seems a better understanding of v. 3 then the RSV, 'elemental spirits', since the contrast Paul develops is between the rudimentary character of the law as compared with the revelation given through Christ.) Slaves in Hellenistic–Roman society could become free sons and heirs only through the legal process of adoption, which entailed an act of redemption which released the former slave from his servitude. This is how we came to be sons and heirs in God's family. He adopted us as sons, satisfying the legal demand for our redemption through the Incarnation and death of His Son (4 f.). When we address Him as 'Father' in response to the encouragement of His Spirit we know we belong to Him as His adopted children and heirs (6 f.). The fact that we have been designated as heirs is due wholly to God (7).

Appreciation of this startling course of events is deepened by the memory of what our past had been. It was characterized by ignorance of our Benefactor and enslavement to the hollow reality of idolatry (8). We faced the prospect only of marking time. God's action in finding us and desiring to know us, not as slaves but as redeemed sons who would enjoy the privilege of knowing Him as only children can know their father, altered our hopeless existence. It is, therefore, inconceivable that we should go back to marking time, even if that time carries the sanction of Mosaic Law (10). The scrupulous observance of Jewish regulations which are rudimentary in character and powerless to alter a man's family standing when we have experienced the redemption of God and the fullness of His revelation (9) would constitute a denial of our new status as sons and heirs. Only thoughtlessness could account for such a reversal in values. Sons have access to the Father, not because they assume the posture of a slave, but because they are sons.

73 : Called to Freedom

Galatians 4.21–5.1

The impossibility of a commitment to both the law and the gospel is expounded in the allegory of Abraham's two sons (4.21–31). The primary reference is to Gen. **16** and **21**.1–21, but Paul's exposition is enriched by other texts drawn from the law and the prophets. His use of allegory to develop the distinction between the old and new covenants (24) may be in response to a method of interpretation used by the Judaizers to discover 'the deeper truths' of Scripture. An allegory implies that the text possesses a meaning distinct from its surface appearance. Paul finds in the text of Gen. **16** and **21** a typical representation of the conflict between law and gospel which prompted his searing letter to the churches of Galatia. The key to the allegory is that he regards Sinai and the Law given there from the perspective of the patriarchal narratives, i.e. from the perspective of promise (23, 28). Ishmael's birth was the result of human cleverness and initiative. He represents those who are convinced that they must come to God with their works in their hands. They therefore embrace law but experience a bondage which is seen in their attachment to works (21, 25). Isaac was born as the result of divine wisdom and initiative in response to faith. He typifies those who are born according to the Spirit (29), who rely on God to achieve His intended ends (28) and so experience freedom. That this applies to Gentile believers Paul shows by Isa. **54**.1, which depicts Jerusalem as a neglected and barren wife who will, however, enjoy a vast increase in children. This prophecy is fulfilled in the gathering of Gentiles into the Church of God (26 f.).

The final part of the exposition focuses on Gen. **21**.9 f. where a sharp distinction is drawn between the son of the slave woman and the son of the free woman who is the true heir (29 f.). Those who submit to the law in response to the human wisdom of the Judaizers will inevitably be separated from the gospel based on the promise and initiative of God. The final verses constitute a clarion call to freedom (**4**.31–**5**.1). Christ broke the yoke of slavery by His death (**5**.1). It is therefore inconceivable that men who have been released from enslavement should ever desire to assume the yoke once again. All the claims of legalism must be resisted by those who have been liberated by Christ. Their heritage is to enjoy responsible freedom in Christ.

74 : Citizens and Sons

Ephesians 2.11–3.6

An occasion for thanksgiving and praise is always provided by a consideration of what God has done. Paul calls his Gentile readers to reflect on the significance of the cross of Christ in their own lives by contrasting their alienated pagan past (11 f.) with their present position in the Church (19–22). Exclusion from the covenant relationship granted to Israel had kept them from a true knowledge of God and had consigned them to a meaningless and hopeless existence. What radically altered this situation was the good news concerning the death of Christ which dealt with the root cause of hostility and alienation—sin. The hostility between Jews and Gentiles found expression in their open disparagement of each other (11). A more tangible symbol of that hostility was the stone barrier erected between the court of the Gentiles and the inner courts of the Temple. An inscription in Greek and Latin prohibited the presence of any Gentile beyond the barrier on penalty of death (cf. Acts **21**.29 f.). When Christ offered Himself as a sacrifice for the sins of the world, He in effect tore down that barrier which separated men from each other (14 f.) and from access to God (18). He thus reconciled Jew and Gentile, for as men are brought near to God they are brought near to each other. The one circumstance in which peace exists horizontally between men and vertically between men and God is the circumstance in which men stand before the cross of Christ (15–18 based on Isa. **57**.19).

This was experienced by Paul's readers. They had been strangers to God's covenant promise and possessed no civic rights in the city of God (12). Now through Christ they possessed the rank of citizens who enjoy the access of sons to the Father as members of the household of faith (18 f.). The image of the household implies an intimate knowledge of God which has displaced their former ignorance of Him. God's household is the place where He dwells, and so the figure of the family merges into that of the holy sanctuary where God manifests His glory (20–22). In view is the Church where Jews and Gentiles enjoy God's indwelling presence through the Holy Spirit. Under the figure of 'the mystery' or 'open secret' (**3**.1–6) Paul declares that it was God's long-hidden surprise that Gentiles should share in the inheritance, the commonwealth and the covenant promises that had belonged exclusively to Israel. God's gracious provision for alienated Gentiles indicates that He confers sonship and inheritance on men who have no claim on Him. From this perspective, sonship and inheritance declare the gospel of the grace of God.

Thought: *A consideration of the 'before' and 'after' of your life in Christ should lead you to the praise of God.*

75 : Suffering and Sonship

Romans 8.14–25

The meaning of sonship is informed by the experience of the Christian in the world. Within this passage Paul associates the world with fear (15), suffering (18), futility (20) and decay (21), which constitute the signs of its fallen condition. It is the realm of death. The action of God in making men sons, as the Holy Spirit applies to them the righteousness secured in Christ, is an affirmation of life. Yet sonship does not exempt believers from being affected by these tokens of death. They must look beyond the immediacy of a moment of anguish to the new creation promised by God (22–25). Hope is anticipation of God's renewal of the creation.

Paul's instruction is a word of assurance. Direction by God's Spirit indicates that Christians enjoy sonship in God's family (14). Sonship leads naturally to assurance, just as fear reduces men to enslavement (15). This is evident in the gatherings of believers for worship. The boldness with which they pray the Lord's Prayer (15, cf. Luke **11**.2) reflects the ministry of the Spirit, persuading them that they are God's children and heirs (15–17). They pray with confidence because they know they have the right to address God as Father. Their position as sons and heirs brings them into relationship with Jesus who is the unique Son and Heir. He is Heir to the glory of God, and believers may anticipate participation in the same inheritance, providing they refuse to dissociate themselves from the sufferings which He endured in the world (17 f.). Paul describes the creation as standing on tiptoe in its impatience for the revealing of the sons of God (19). This implies that, to the onlooker, it is not completely evident now who are and who are not sons, but that this will be revealed when Christ returns to complete His work of renewal. For in spite of the intrusion of death into the created order, the cycle of birth—decay—rebirth in the changing of the seasons excited the hope of a time when bondage to decay would be past in the renewal of the creation by God (20–21). Now creation and men join in a chorus of groans from which even those who are sons and heirs to glory are not removed, for our bodies experience the decay of the natural order (22 f.). Yet the willingness of the Holy Spirit to join that chorus of sorrow as He identifies Himself with our suffering (26 f.) assures us that God's renewing work will extend even to our bodies. We know that the hope which entered our lives when Christ made us sons and heirs cannot be false. The impatience of the world (19) finds its counterpoint in the patience of sons (24 f.) who wait for God to complete His perfect work.

Thought: *The coming of Jesus Christ signals the rebirth of hope.*

Questions and themes for study and discussion on Studies 69–75

1. If sonship is a reflection of the father, what qualities of God the Father must be reflected in our lives?
2. In contemporary society liberation movements command considerable attention. How does Jesus' statement in John **8**.36 influence a Christian's response to these several expressions of a cry for freedom?
3. Why do forms of legalism always creep into Christian communities? What is the cost of legalism and of responsible freedom?
4. What can we learn about the privileges of our sonship to God by reflecting on the meaning of sonship in our own families? Will we want to change our relationship to our children after we reflect on God's relationship to us?
5. How does Christian hope transform the experience of suffering? How should we define the content of Christian hope? Why is sonship the prerequisite for enduring hope?

CHARACTER STUDIES

76 : The Crowd

John 7.17–44; 8.54–59; 11.54–57; 12.12–19

All through John's Gospel there is a consciousness of the crowd, the faceless multitude which was a force and a presence in Palestine in the first century. The crowd, in fact, has been a feature in all history. This day has seen it—the forest of uplifted arms under the swastikas at Nuremberg, the horde chanting war slogans before the Palazzo Venezia, thronging Red Square and the streets of Peking. The crowd can be a force, ruthless and cruel in the hands of demagogue and dictator. Wind and wave can combine to form an irresistible force. So can the gales of emotion which sweep through crowds and peoples, and change a group of human beings into a destroying mass, yelling for Barabbas, overwhelming the good around an uplifted cross, obliterating the higher scruples of individuals . . .

Jerusalem was fearfully crowded at festival times, and the occupying forces, as well as the collaborating hierarchy, were well aware of the latent power of the crowd. Well they might be! It was a crowd manifesting in its collective personality the worst features of Jewish nationalism, hate and fierce anger, that precipitated the clash in A.D. 66, and the awful rebellion which followed. It needed only the explosive injection of Galilean turbulence, or the fiery words of some demagogue to set Jerusalem in an uproar.

In John **7** we sense the presence of the Jerusalem multitude. They were unsure of the nature of the new teaching which was abroad, confused and incoherent. The 'murmuring' (12, AV [KJV]) which is a better rendering than the 'muttering' of the RSV, suggests the buzz of discussion and speculation which the rulers (26) dreaded to hear canalize into a roar of loyalty like that of the Ephesian mob (Acts **19**.28). They were to hear the chanting of Palm Sunday with deep anxiety, and, had the Lord been a mob-leader, that day could have seen riot and rebellion. To this point, however, the crowd was pitiable, without leaders rather than misled, unconscious of the power which makes the mob the tool of evil, 'sheep without a shepherd'. Again and again we see the Lord refuse to use the multitude. 'He knew what was in man.' He knew that the crowd could blot out individuality, and that man's decisions were not made under the force of gregarious instinct, but by individual thought and committal (17). They were left divided (43) because this was inevitable. They had to come to Him as men and women, not a tramping horde.

77 : The Officers

John 7.45, 46; 18.1–8

Here was a strange excuse for a group of disciplined guards sent on a specific errand. They could not arrest Him 'because no man spoke as He spoke'. As strange and as significant was the fact that the excuse was virtually accepted. The Sanhedrin realized that some unnatural power surrounded the person of Christ. In their blind hostility they refused to call it a supernatural power, but it was of this that they were aware, and, in spite of angry words, they received the report of the Temple guard.

Who were these men? The Jerusalem hierarchy, in return for the quite invaluable aid and comfort which their collaboration gave to the Roman garrison and occupying forces, had certain privileges. One of them was that they were in charge of the Temple area and its national sanctity. A notice survives which threatens death to any intruder from outside Jewry, who might presume to intrude on the sacred parts of the Temple complex. In the support of this privilege the Sanhedrin had at its disposal a police or para-military force which was used to effect the arrest of Christ. With the deterioration of the political position on Palestine, and thanks to the Roman desire to avoid all provocation in the tense situation, the Sanhedrin doubtless presumed on the powers they had. The stoning of Stephen was an illustration.

Who were the components of this force? We can identify the wounded man of Gethsemane, Malchus, the servant of the high priest (John **18**.10). They were all Jews, though for special tasks some officer of the Roman garrison in the fortress Antonia might perhaps have been attached to the force. They were probably young Levites, with access to the

Temple, picked and paid by the ruling Sadducees, men conditioned to obey orders, and owing all they had or could hope for to the ruling caste. Hence the remarkable nature of the situation when, daunted by the words of Christ, or apprehensive of the crowd, they were paralysed in the prosecution of their duty. And catch the reflection of the tremendous personality of Christ; no despised Galilean, no desert hermit, no defenceless weakling, but a Being of elemental power in word and presence.

78 : Nicodemus

John 3.1–3; 7.50–53; 19.39–42

Christians who know the inside of a University common room will find something grimly familiar in the little picture of Nicodemus and the doctors of the law (7.50–53). Picking up the contemptible remark of v. 49, the learned Pharisee speaks to his colleagues of their own contempt of the Law. They silence him on an academic point. Jonah, in fact, came from Galilee. But was Jonah, with his mission to the Gentiles, to be listed as a prophet? Too cautious to argue and to commit himself in such an environment, Nicodemus lapses into silence.

Writing recently of C. S. Lewis, Mr. George Bailey remarked: 'As a popularizer of Christian dogma, Lewis was embarrassing to the academic community . . . I never heard Lewis, nor anyone else—including the college chaplain—discuss his religious works at Oxford . . . For the university, Lewis's standing as a scholar was checkmated by his unwelcome fame as an apologist of Christianity'. Many Christians of academic eminence, know how nearly impossible it is to overcome this ingrained and altogether ignorant prejudice by the worth of their instruction or by the value of their secular contributions to scholarship. The 'offence of the cross' must still be borne. The remedy for the burden is to look steadfastly at the students who watch and depend.

It is difficult to assess Nicodemus in the situation of this chapter. Says Leon Morris: 'The temper of the meeting must be borne in mind. Plain testimony to Jesus would undoubtedly have enraged the majority further. Nicodemus may have judged that Christ's cause might best be served by pointing these angry men to a legal weakness in their position'.

J. C. Ryle commends Nicodemus: 'Slow work is sometimes the surest and most enduring . . . No doubt it would be a pleasant thing if everyone who was converted came out boldly, took up the cross, and confessed Christ on the day of his conversion. But it is not always given to God's children to do so . . . Better a little grace than none. Better move slowly than stand still in sin and the world'. But how true it all is to life!

79 : The Adulteress

John 3.17–21; 8.1–11

In the RSV the story of the woman in the Temple court is relegated to a footnote. There is a considerable number of ancient manuscripts which omit it. It is undoubtedly part of the Christian tradition and a genuine part of Scripture. It may be the work of another hand and attached by John to his manuscript. This would account for stylistic differences, very difficult to nail down. And the wide omission of the story could have been due to a growing deviation in the Church, and the emergence of asceticism.

It is vividly written. We can see the surge of activity round the bowed and silent figure. 'Here she is, Rabbi, caught in the act. Now the Law of Moses, not our additions to the Law, which are your constant theme of criticism, but the Lawgiver's own solemn enactment, is clear enough. Now, pray, your opinion?' He bent down, and with His finger made marks in the sand on the flagstones.

They continued importunately. He looked up, and said: 'Let the one without sin among you be the first to throw the stone'. Observe the definite article. 'Surely, in a group so dedicated to the Law, there must be one without any sin at all!' He continued writing, and there must be some vital significance in what He wrote. And whatever it was He wrote, those who watched were convicted by their conscience and 'began to slip away one by one, beginning with the eldest down to the last'.

The order of preference is very curious, and may be the

key to the understanding of the incident. Did He, in the mysterious writing, communicate something shocking, ironically following the order of seniority of which the hierarchy was so fond? Did the eldest stone-thrower see a name emerging?—'But she is dead, dead this twenty years'. He drops his stone and slips away. Another sees a date, one long banished from his mind. Another reads: 'Ephesus'. Yes, Ephesus, does He know? The temple of Diana? That woman? No Jew saw me, but He knows'—He drops his stone. Something like this made them go.

But note the awful fact that such conviction was not in any sense salutary. It stirred no desire for salvation, only for escape. No one stepped forward, knelt by the cowering woman, and craved pardon. All they desired in their hard and hate-filled lives was to escape the presence of the One who had hit hard on their crust of self-esteem. Like things of darkness which fear the light, they shrink back into the murk, lest the hidden corners be exposed and disinfected.

80 : The Adulterer

John 8.12–44

And so they sought to slip away into their guilty anonymity. They were not very successful. They confronted holiness, felt its light penetrate their darkened characters, and fled. Each Pharisee knew, too, that the others guessed the reason for the flight, and if no one remarked upon the fact, it was because of a tacit partnership of silence. In the whole scene there is one person alone who successfully covered his escape. We cannot even prescribe a verse in which to read about him, or on which to build some description of his person.

He is the figure missing from the vivid story, the man who found no forgiveness, as did his pathetic companion in sin. She was, according to her captors, taken 'in the very act'. There was therefore a man 'taken in adultery', who was not dragged, like the woman, into the presence of Christ. We can only guess how he was involved, and how he came to cover his cowardly escape, and to leave his associate in sin to face the consequences. Was he nimble of foot, influential, rich? Whatever the means of his escape, it could not be permanent. Guilt is a grim companion, and guilt ran off with its host. Nor is that the end. There is a judgement at the last, and no evil ultimately escapes.

No sin can be successfully confined to the place and time of its committing. Few sins can be held within the area of the person who commits them. Sin is commonly a partnership. If not that, it is an infection, too readily passed on. No person can live independently, and how often has that awesome and challenging truth emerged in these studies of the characters of Scripture. Someone persuaded the woman to sin, or even if she was the temptress we met in Proverbs, someone met her seduction with response and not rebuke, and sealed her guilt with opportunity. Someone could have said no, or helped a weakling to say no to temptation. Someone thought he had escaped, would hear no more of the doings of a shameful hour, and someone outside or behind this story made the tragic error which millions have repeated, for 'the Day shall reveal it'. It could be today.

81 : The Man Born Blind

John 9.1–12

John, as we have seen, often chooses his stories because of the significance of the events or the words consequential upon them. Sometimes a brevity of narrative results, and details require explanation. The RSV repeats the error of its predecessors in v. 3 and makes the words imply that a man was born blind in order that forty years later a miracle might be performed. It should be remembered that in ancient writing there were no punctuation marks or even divisions between words and sentences. Consequently, misunderstandings have sometimes arisen. There should be a fullstop in the middle of v. 3, and no stop at its end. The reply will then run: 'Neither did this man sin nor his parents. But that the works of God may be made manifest in him, we must work the works of Him that sent me while it is day. The night comes, when no man can work.' In other words, faced with the spectacle of human pain, the Lord first rebuts the doctrine that has found so large place in Eastern thought, that all suffering is of our own making, and then stresses the Christian fact that all need is a call to action in God's name with faith and urgency. The power that wrought the miracle was all His own. The promptitude with which He gave His help is an example we all can follow.

And in the same story why the peculiar method of the cure? Was this a concession to superstition? No, not in the sense that He Himself was the victim of a superstition. He was gloriously free from all such mental malady. But it is, perhaps, possible that the blind man may have held the popular belief that the spittle of a good man possesses healing power. It was necessary to help his faith. The Lord's miracles were a type of all salvation. The act of grace availed only when faith, however weak, met it with response. The blind beggar had little knowledge of God. The tags of popular theology which he uses in his clever duel with the Pharisees are witness enough to that. Somehow faith must awaken in his soul, if the miracle of healing is to take place. That is why the Lord steps on to his plane. He performs an act which rouses a spark of hope in the man's soul. Then He asks the man to do something with faith. The psychology is perfect. He who knew the soul of the man knew how the blind man's mind would work. With hope fanning a fire of faith in his heart, the blind man groped his way to the Pool of Siloam, 'and came back seeing'. Neither the clay nor the water of the pool had healing powers, but both were the agents which stimulated the faith which saved him.

82 : The Man Who Saw

John 9.13–41

The character of the man who received his sight emerges with some vividness from John's account of the interview with the Sanhedrin. The story bears all the marks of being an eye-witness account. John appears to have had access to the high-priest's house, and, as appears from the story of Peter by the fire, the proceedings of the Sanhedrin could be heard from the courtyard, into which those who could pass the doorkeeper could penetrate.

Observe the wary brevity with which the man tells the story (cf. vs. 11, 15). He does not betray a name to potential foes of his benefactor. He replies with studied economy of words. Like his canny parents, he has learned in the hard school of the slum and the city gate, that it is a good thing in a hostile situation to give away as little as possible. He has learned, too, not to look for help from anybody. From the two dour parents the man certainly has little help. They gave priority to the preservation of their own security.

Dorothy Sayers, in her famous broadcast radio play on the story of Christ (*The Man Born to be King,* 1943), caught the humour of the debate very well. Even in the brief Gospel story it emerges, especially when the man catches up the confident 'we know' of the priests, who had allowed themselves to be drawn into undignified argument in their frustration.

Dorothy Sayers made her Jacob say: 'Well now, that's a queer thing, ain't it? You don't know where the man comes from—and yet he knew how to open my eyes. He's a bad man, you say. All right. Does God hear the prayers of bad people? "No," says you, "of course He don't." Does He hear the prayers of good people? "Yes," you say, "He does." Well, look 'ee here. Here's a thing never heard on since the world began, that somebody should open the eyes of a man that was born blind. Nobody can't do a thing like that, only by God's help. Stands to reason.'

Read the chapter, trying to visualize the scene—the lofty theologians, the earthy ignorant man who doggedly held to the facts of his experience. The dramatist has given the flavour. One can imagine the zest with which John, who had slipped away to listen, retailed the story.

83 : The Blind Leaders

Isaiah 42.6, 7, 18–20; 44.18–20; 53.1–3; John 9.39–41

John had told the story of the blind man, not only for the relish of the Sanhedrin debate, but to set down the Lord's remark about the blindness of the soul. It is one of the commonest figures of speech in the Bible. There are those with eyes who cannot see. The rulers 'saw no beauty' in Christ. It is part of the quickening which comes with the life Christ gives that all that which the physical vision commands becomes more meaningful.

'Lord, what a lovely thing the moon is', Dorothy Sayers makes her Jacob say, 'to think I never saw it till last night'. George Wade Robinson caught up the same thought:

Something lives in every hue
Christless eyes have never seen.

Vision is a quality of the mind. How much do we truly see without involvement of the mind and the insights of the spirit? The animal sees but does not comprehend. Man takes the message of the eye, its report of line and hue, and relates it to another world, another dimension of understanding. Hence all poetry, all joy in beauty, all those deeper levels of awareness which make man different from the animal. Those whom Christ chided for their blindness, were unable in the grip of pride, amid the preoccupations of looking on themselves, and through the crassness of their self-willed corruption, to see the movement of the hand of God in their critical days, and above all to see in Christ the message God gave, the last and fullest revelation of Himself. He had nothing else to reveal. If men, in deliberate obstinacy, persisted in seeing in Him only the harried preacher from Galilee, the pathetic visionary, the peril to their comfort—God had no more to show. Blind to Him, they were blind to all.

Questions and themes for study and discussion on Studies 76–83

1. The cost of being a Christian.
2. How does one deal with hostility at home?
3. What would it be like personally to confront the living Christ? How, in fact, is He still confronted?
4. The academic cult of 'suspended judgement'.
5. When is conviction of sin salutary?
6. 'Sin is commonly committed in partnership'.
7. What do we learn concerning our contact with individuals from Christ's treatment of the blind man?

RIGHTEOUSNESS IN CHRIST

Assurance of Salvation

84 : The Enjoyment of Life

John 3.31–36; 5.24; 6.35–40

In response to the faith which appropriates the righteousness in Christ God assures men of their salvation. The term is rich in meaning, but salvation speaks of rescue from death and the wrath of God merited by disobedience, and also the enjoyment of life in God's presence. Salvation makes itself known and felt in the present, but it will be completely disclosed only in the future when God gathers His people to Himself. The solid foundation of a believer's assurance of salvation is the solemn promise of God who is true (**3**.33).

In John's Gospel Jesus is the 'Sent One'. He was sent into the world to utter the Father's words (**3**.34) and to do His will (**6**.38 f.). The fullness of the Spirit which He enjoys guarantees the truthfulness of His word, while the extent of His commission (authority over 'all things') shows how deeply the Father loves the Son (**3**.34–35). So the One who came from the Father's presence, Jesus, is uniquely qualified to disclose the intention of God (**3**.31 f.; **6**.38). That intention is announced in the parallel statements of **3**.36 and **5**.24. The alternating expressions 'eternal life' and 'wrath of God' (**3**.36) indicate that Jesus is speaking of salvation. Faith in God's Son secures for the believer the assurance of 'life'. 'Eternal life' contemplates the life which is promised in terms of its quality and duration. The life God gives to His people is the life that He Himself enjoys. It is so qualitatively different from the life ordinarily enjoyed by men that it can be described in terms of resurrection, the dramatic experience of life from the dead (**5**.24). The bestowal of this life now through the Son anticipates His work of raising the dead at the end of the age (**6**.38–40). Participation in eternal life following the resurrection will hinge on the possession of eternal life now. For those who respond to Jesus' word of invitation with unbelief there remains only the expectation of judgement (**5**.24) and wrath (**3**.36). Unbelief is characterized as disobedience because it manifests that contempt for God which first separated men from God in the Garden (Gen. **3**). It merits God's wrath because it refuses to respect God's provision for life when disobedience permitted the intrusion of death. Between the enjoyment of life and the experience of wrath there is no middle ground. Response to Jesus determines a man's earthly and eternal destiny. The one who trusts Jesus will experience the full comfort of His word of assurance: he will enjoy full satisfaction (**6**.35), loving acceptance (**6**.37) and absolute security (**6**.39 f.).

85 : Safety

John 10.1–30

Under the figure of the shepherd and the sheepfold Jesus spoke of the relationship between Himself and His people. The extended simile draws its material from first-century practice. Palestinian sheepfolds were usually walled enclosures with a single gate. Several shepherds would drive their flocks into a single sheepfold, leaving them in the care of an under-shepherd. After the gate was secured from the inside, he would remain with the sheep all night. In the morning he would admit the shepherds, so that each could call away his own sheep. In the North East, where the intimacy between shepherd and sheep is close, the naming of sheep is a very ancient practice. The sheep naturally recognized the shepherd's voice and distinguished it from that of a stranger (1–5). By this figurative language Jesus indicated to hostile Pharisees (cf. **9**.24–41) His own relationship to those who responded enthusiastically to His teaching (cf. **7**.31, 40, 46–49).

His expansion of the simile draws on the fact that the shepherd stood in the entrance to the sheepfold, forming a door which permitted the sheep to pass one by one, so that he could inspect them. He was their door to safety, freedom and satisfaction of their needs, and the life of the sheep depended on his concern for them. Response to his voice, following his leading, entrance into the fold through him, and the refusal to follow others was for the sheep the condition of security. Jesus applied the figure of the shepherd as the door (7, 9) to Himself to indicate that this is the condition of our safety as well.

The contrast between the thief who *takes* life (1, 8, 10) and the shepherd who *protects* life (9) is sharpened by Jesus' teaching that He is the good Shepherd who *gives* life (11, 14). Wild beasts and armed bands were a serious threat to the safety of a flock. While a hired gatekeeper might sacrifice his charge to save his life (12 f.), the good shepherd is the one who saves his charge, even at the cost of his own life (11–15, 17–18, 28). This distinction between the hireling and the good shepherd points up the crucial significance of Jesus' death to our salvation. Jesus' statement, however, goes beyond the figure of the faithful shepherd who is ready to die for his sheep. His ability to take up His life again (17 f.) foreshadows His resurrection and explains why He is the source of eternal life to all who come to God through Him (27 f.). His death and resurrection are the measure of the Father's love for His people and constitute the pledge of their security, for on the question of commitment to believers and of power exercised on their behalf Jesus and the Father are one (18, 27–30).

Thought: *Even as Jesus is the Good Shepherd, those who have responsibility in the Church of God must be good shepherds.*

86 : Assured through Love

Romans 8.28–39; 2 Timothy 1.8–14

Assured conviction frequently flows from thoughtful reflection. Rom. 8.23–39 is an exalted meditation on the purpose and power of God's love. Christians are the special objects of God's unfolding purpose, for He has destined us to share the family likeness even as we enjoy the privilege of family fellowship (28 f.). The love we bring to God is a direct response to His love expressed toward us in Christ, a love which is contemplated under the headings of foreknowledge, calling, justification and glorification (30). As a father knows and loves his child before his child comes to know and love him, so God knew and loved His children. 'Calling' points to the moment when we recognized God's love for us. 'Justification' embraces the whole life of faith but anticipates the judgement when the verdict 'justified' will have ultimate significance for us. 'Glorification' is God's crowning achievement as He bestows on His family the glory displayed in Jesus Christ (18). Reflection on this uninterrupted flow of love stirs Paul to the praise of God who rescued Christians from a just condemnation (31–34) and made them invincible in the presence of suffering and death through His unconditional love (35–39). These verses may preserve for us an inspired hymn to the power of God's love.

The firm persuasion that 'God is for us' (31) is the sufficient base of Christian confidence. His willingness to sacrifice His Son for all the redeemed was the supreme expression of His love, and guarantees that all good gifts will be added to this best gift (31 f., cf. v. 28 'all things'). When the adversary will accuse God's children in the judgement, Christ will be their advocate who will plead the sufficient satisfaction of every demand by their Saviour (33 f.). The intercession of the Son is the assurance that the Christian never needs to fear condemnation (cf. v. 1). Neither accusation for past sin nor the threat to life posed by acute suffering can shake the Christian's assurance that he is loved by God and has been marked out for salvation. Conformity to Christ (29) implies the experience of suffering in the world (17 f.), and suffering becomes meaningful when we are abused because we are identified with Christ (35–37; 2 Tim. **1**.8–12). Even those demonic powers which enslave and tyrannize life are powerless before the love of God, for Christ has triumphed over them (38 f., cf. Col. **2**.15; Eph. **1**.21–23), and in Him we experience the exultant joy of victory (38 f.). The assurance of salvation, based on the triumphant lordship of Christ, releases us to willing acceptance of suffering and responsible stewardship in the world (2 Tim. **1**.12–14).

Thought: *Predestination means—among other things—that we know where we are going before we get there.*

87 : The Peril of Apostasy

Hebrews 6

This exceedingly solemn word of warning must not be heard in a merely academic way. Our response must reflect the deep earnestness of the writer, who prepared for what he says in **6**.4 ff. by exposing the scandal of immaturity in his readers.

They had failed to appreciate the importance of moral decision to Christian maturity, and so were 'unskilled in the word of righteousness' (**5**.11–14). In the second century 'the word of righteousness' was a recognized phrase in the preparation of believers for martyrdom, suggesting that this was something the unskilled were not prepared for. This interpretation explains the deep concern the writer displays over the readers' immaturity, and why he immediately turns to consider the peril of apostasy (**6**.4–8). The cost of discipleship could give a man second thoughts about identifying himself with Jesus (cf. Mark **8**.34–38; **14**.66–72). Maturity obtained in the arena of decision-making will prepare a man for the moment when an ultimate decision for Christ must be made. Conversely, immaturity and indecisiveness may be the prelude to a radical rejection of Jesus.

There is an element of mystery in the outworking of God's permissive will. Nevertheless, the hard reality of apostasy must be recognized. It entails a deliberate renunciation of Jesus Christ which exposes Him to contempt before men and confirms the world in its unbelief (**6**.6, cf. **10**.26–31). Pliny the Younger in a letter to the emperor Trajan spoke of some Christians 'forsaking Jesus and cursing Him'. Apostasy is directed against Jesus' person and against the efficacy of His sacrifice on the cross. Because it is committed wilfully and habitually (the tenses of the verbs in **10**.26 ff. are important as bringing this out) it entails personal responsibility for the consequences of this refusal of God's provision of righteousness. Such a person cannot be restored to repentance (**6**.4) for he has repudiated the ground on which repentance may be offered to men, the death of Jesus, and has rejected God's grace extended in Christ. Exposure to God's gifts (5) demands an appropriate response (7 f.). The question posed by **6**.4–8, therefore, is this: what is the issue of your life?

We need to be reminded of the reality of responsibility in the Christian life, for we have a holy God who has provided a costly redemption. A rejection of His provision for salvation leaves to men only the fierce expectation of judgement, as they confront the fiery indignation of God (**10**.26–31). Apostasy deserves this judgement. Radical rejection of the Lord brings in its wake radical rejection by Him (cf. Mark **8**.38). Yet the God who speaks so severely, speaks in this way precisely because He loves us! His concern and compassion in setting forth this warning are evident. It is a fearful thing to fall into the hands of the living God (**10**.31). But for those who flee to Him for refuge (**6**.18) in a time when men are pressed to be untrue to Him there is no experience of terror but of encouragement. Among the encouragements offered by the writer to us are the certainty of God's remembrance of past faithfulness (**6**.9 f.) and the assurance of God's assistance (**6**.13–20). His desire is to show convincingly the unchangeable character of His purpose for us (17), for it is impossible that He should prove false (18). The focus of our hope remains Jesus the Forerunner, whose priestly ministry on our behalf assures us that our anticipation of salvation is unshaken in spite of the turbulence of persecution and martyrdom (19 f.).

Thought: The gospel consists of grace and truth: grace *that we should not despair;* truth *that we should not presume on God.*

88 : Sin and Forgiveness

1 John 1

Fellowship with God and with others who know Him through Christ is an essential ingredient in Christian living. When God brings persons close to Himself, He brings them close to each other. In this pastoral letter fellowship is a primary concern to John. He writes as an eyewitness to the reality of the Incarnation who had enjoyed intimate fellowship with Jesus. His purpose in writing is to lay a firm foundation for an extension of Christian fellowship and joy (1–4). This letter may have served to introduce the Gospel of John (cf. v. 2 with John **1**.1–18) but its primary concerns are practical, the enjoyment of unbroken fellowship with the Father and the Son (3).

A major threat to fellowship is the reality of sin in the lives of believers. Sin always separates men from God and each other. The threat of disruption is vividly presented through the imagery of light and darkness. John knows that the basis of fellowship must be more substantial than the mouthing of correct phrases. The message that 'God is light' (5) is an abstract truth which was also believed by heretical teachers and many pagans. John, therefore, works out the implications of this truth with reference to righteousness (**1**.5–**2**.6) and love (**2**.7–17). His point is that doctrinal affirmation must be tested by an ethical demand, so that faith and conduct are harmonious (6 f.). If God is light, we must walk in the light of His truth or forfeit the privilege of His fellowship.

Yet realism demands the recognition of sin in the lives of Christians. John labels the attempt to deny this fact as a lying deception which dishonours God (8, 10). Fellowship must consequently depend on God's ability to deal with the problem of persisting sin. His response to this problem displays His own righteousness. The question of sin was settled by Jesus' perfect obedience which satisfied every demand of God's righteousness (7). Because Jesus is able to plead His death on behalf of sinners, forgiveness and cleansing from the effects of sin are consistent with God's justice (9). Our response must be confession and repentance, in confident reliance on the Sacrifice which made a just forgiveness possible. The message of life is that we have been forgiven and are being forgiven. The experience of renewed forgiveness and cleansing through Jesus' blood assures us of that ultimate forgiveness which seals to us our salvation.

Thought: *The Church must be the place where sin is confessed and forgiveness is expressed in Christian love.*

89 : Responsible Love

1 John 2.1–14

It is imperative that we never presume on the forgiveness of God. The gospel knows nothing of cheap grace, but only of the costly grace of forgiveness purchased through Jesus' suffering and death on the cross. The promise of full forgiveness and cleansing (**1**.7, 9) must not become an excuse for surrender to sin. John's real intention is to lead his people, whom he addresses affectionately as his dear children, beyond the experience of continual humiliation by sin. He knows, nevertheless, that the accusing reality of sin can erect a barrier that keeps us from receiving God's forgiveness. He therefore stresses the strong intercessory ministry of 'the Righteous One', whose atoning death enables Him to plead effectively for us (1 f.). Forgiveness, however, is never an end in itself. Its goal is to release men to that obedience to God which demonstrates that they know Him and love Him (3–6). The knowledge of God, deepened by the experience of forgiveness and fellowship, imposes on men a binding obligation to regard His commandments seriously.

The commandment that John has particularly in mind is Jesus' instruction to love one another (cf. John **13**.34). That is an old commandment found in the Holiness Code (Lev. **19**.18) but it had been infused with newness when Jesus made His love for His disciples the measure of the love they were to show to each other. The new commandment was given substance when Jesus laid down His life for His people. It must now be given substance by Christians, since Jesus had said that men would know they were His followers by the love they displayed to each other (John **13**.35). This means that the existence of hostility in a church member poses a disturbing question mark over his claim to know Jesus. Only those who reflect the light of Christ's love may be confident of His approval when they appear before Him. Hatred interferes with a man's vision of the will of God (9–11). By using the device of repetition, John establishes his point emphatically (12–14). He speaks first to all believers ('little children'), and then in turn to the more mature ones ('fathers') and to those in their prime ('young men'), reviewing the privileges of sonship they have enjoyed. Forgiveness of sins, knowledge of the Father and power over the evil one through life in the Son impose the responsibility to reflect His love in our relationship to each other. Responsible Christian love among brethren makes Jesus visible in the world and proves that we belong to Him (6).

Thought: Forgiveness imposes a debt of love which we discharge by extending forgiveness to others.

90 : Children of God

1 John 3

There is a certain hiddenness that characterizes God's children. Although we have been adopted into God's family, to the world we look no different. John eagerly anticipates the day when the family resemblance between God and His children will be apparent to all. At Christ's coming we shall be transformed by the vision of God in Christ so as 'to be like him' (1 f.). While we wait for that moment of glory the hope of that bodily transformation encourages in us a moral transformation, so that God's purity becomes the goal of our lives (3).

Reflection on the revealing of God's children in the future (1–3) leads John to speak of the revealing of God's Son in the past (4–8) and of His children in the present (7–10). John reserves the term 'Son' for Jesus (cf. John **3**.16, 'His unique Son'), choosing to refer to Christians as 'children'. The statements that the Son of God *appeared* in the world (cf. **1**.1–3) to 'take away sins' (5) and 'to destroy the works of the devil' (8) have in view the work accomplished by Jesus in His death (cf. John **1**.29; **12**.31). Consequently, the distinction between the family of God and the family of the devil has now *become apparent* (10), for the children of God are not characterized by the commission of sin (6–9).

Inevitably the sharp formulation of vs. 6–9 raises two questions: 'Is a Christian unable to sin?' and 'If I sin, can I call myself a Christian?' These verses cannot be considered apart from the equally emphatic statements in **1**.8 and **2**.1, which frankly recognize the sins of believers. In **3**.6–9 John draws on the significance of the present tense, which speaks of continuation in an action. More important, he insists that the new birth makes a difference; it produces fruit in the life. Though a believer may fall into sin, God does not regard him as one who lives in sin. He is distinguished from one who is a child of the devil by a righteous love for his brothers (7, 10).

Such a love rules out hatred (11–15). The commandment of love is thrown into bold relief by contrast with its opposite (cf. John **10**.15; **15**.13). Like Jesus, John defines hatred as murder (cf. Matt. **5**.22) and traces its source to the devil (cf. John **8**.44). A life of Christian love, however, will imitate Jesus by a preparedness to lay down our lives for our brothers in Christ (16–18). While the language is appropriate to martyrdom, John has in mind primarily that self-denial which moves us to share our material possessions with those in need (17). A love which fails to find expression in openhearted compassion obscures the love which moved God to send His Son into the world. Yet, when we do act lovingly toward others, we experience the assurance that our actions are prompted by God and that we belong to Him (19–24). This is not something automatic, for we do have guilt feelings (20a), but we are led to the conviction that God is greater than our feelings and we can trust Him (20b). If we experience no feelings of guilt, it is because we have fully trusted Jesus Christ and have sought to love one another, while the response of God is the presence of His Spirit assuring us of His abiding love.

Thought: *Love is not a vague, abstract quality, but a reality manifested with regard to the most commonplace and practical matters.*

91 : A Life of Assurance

1 John 4.13–5.3; 5.13–21

Like a concert organist at the conclusion of a recital, John pulls out all the stops as he brings together the themes of Christian assurance and responsibility developed in the course of the letter. The Spirit of God confirms both the reality of our Christian life (13) and the truth of the gospel (14–16), so that we are able to acknowledge with our lives that Jesus is the Son of God and the Saviour of the world. When we consider the meaning of Jesus in our lives, we understand and accept with thanksgiving the love that God has for us (16). With tenderness John develops this, though in terms of the opposition between love and fear (17–19). The assurance that God loves us is our confidence as we anticipate what it will mean to stand before Him on the day of judgement. The knowledge that we have offended God's majesty and holiness is sufficient to awaken within us the fear of punishment (18). But God's perfect love in identifying us with Christ (17) forcefully addresses and exorcises our fear. We respond with a love called forth by the magnitude of His boundless love (19) as an echo answers the shout of the voice. What is distinctive of John's emphasis is his pastoral concern to channel the love we bring to God, so that it flows through the Church. God has loved us and we can return that love to Him by loving our brothers in the Lord (**4**.20–**5**.3).

In the closing segment of the letter (**5**.13–21) John sustains the note of assurance in order to end on the note of responsibility. As John **20**.31 states the purpose of his Gospel, v. 13 discloses the purpose of his Epistle: God intends us to be aware of our salvation. Earlier the apostle defined salvation as a victory over the world achieved by Jesus and claimed through faith by Christians (**5**.4 f., cf. John **16**.33). Participation in that victory is now considered as the assurance of answered prayer (14–17). The sole limitations placed on boldness in prayer are submission to God's will (14) and the recognition that there is a mortal sin which defies God so callously that prayer is ineffective (16). Prayer is considered primarily in the context of church discipline (16–18); it is an effective means for restoring men to fellowship with the Father. There is a final assurance of victory over the world and 'the evil one' with the help of 'the True One' and His Son. This prepares for the solemn charge to a life which resolutely turns away from every illusion that threatens to usurp the place reserved for the reality of God (18–21). God is found revealed in Jesus Christ alone. His fidelity assures us of our salvation.

Questions and themes for study and discussion on Studies 84–91

1. How will you explain the meaning of salvation to someone who has no knowledge of Jesus or Scripture?
2. Does the assurance of salvation encourage spiritual carelessness or moral laxity? What is lost if these expressions of thoughtlessness are found in a Christian's life?
3. Is all suffering in the life of a Christian 'for the sake of Christ'? What is implied by that qualifying phrase? Can one who never suffers for Christ have the assurance of salvation?
4. Is a sense of guilt a tool of God or of Satan? Should such a sense ever be allowed to destroy a Christian's confidence in his salvation?
5. What substitutes for God pose a continual threat to Christian fidelity? How will the admonition from idols be translated in our own lives?